One
Simple Idea
for
Startups
and
Entrepreneurs

One Simple Idea

for
Startups
and
Entrepreneurs

**Live Your Dreams and
Create Your Own Profitable Company**

STEPHEN KEY
with Colleen Sell

New York   Chicago   San Francisco   Lisbon   London   Madrid   Mexico City
Milan   New Delhi   San Juan   Seoul   Singapore   Sydney   Toronto

1 2 3 4 5 6 7 8 9 0   QFR/QFR   1 8 7 6 5 4 3 2

ISBN   978-0-07-180044-0
MHID   0-07-180044-1

e-ISBN 978-0-07-180045-7
e-MHID   0-07-180045-X

McGraw-Hill books are available at special quantity discounts to use as
premiums and sales promotions or for use in corporate training programs.
To contact a representative, please e-mail us at bulksales@mcgraw-hill.com.

This book is printed on acid-free paper.

To my fathers:

James Leslie Key, for teaching me many of the basic business principles that have made me a success. He took a lot of the guesswork and mystery out of starting and running a business.

John Gordon Kimball, for supporting me emotionally, challenging me mentally, being my mentor, and pouring a great cocktail every Friday night for 20 years!

Contents

Preface

Who Is Taylor Swift?

Iᴛ ʜᴀᴘᴘᴇɴᴇᴅ in the summer of 2007, and I remember it well. I left for lunch early, at a little after eleven, like I always did. My business, Hot Picks, was taking off, and I was adamant that someone remain in the office to answer the phone at all times. Customer service has always been of utmost importance to me, and that summer the phone was constantly ringing. So it was James, my assistant for more than a decade, who answered the call that took us to a place I'd never dreamed we would be. When I walked through the office door an hour later, James had a peculiar look on his face.

"Steve," he said, "You won't believe who called."

We were getting calls from a lot of different people at that point, so I wasn't sure what to expect.

"It was Scott Swift!" He looked so excited.

The name didn't register. "James, who is Scott Swift?" I asked.

"Taylor Swift's dad!" he declared triumphantly.

"Who is Taylor Swift?"

Looking back, it seems a little bit ludicrous that I had never heard of Taylor Swift. I try to keep up with what's hip (and I like to think that I do an okay job at it). I was working in the music business. Taylor Swift was quickly becoming hugely popular. My friends, my wife, and my kids all knew who she was. What do I know? I'm 51! She just wasn't on my radar screen.

The next thing I knew, I was working with Scott Swift to produce lenticular picks of Taylor strumming her guitar, long blond tresses flowing. A few months later, I took my family backstage to meet her and her mother at one of her concerts. There's a photo of my son and Taylor on our refrigerator to this day. It's been a few years since then, and the experience still feels surreal because it *was*.

When my partner and I first started Hot Picks, I would spend Saturday mornings packaging my guitar picks at the kitchen table with my wife and kids. I can still see the picks strewn out across the surface of the table we ate dinner on every night, and fallen skulls and devils and aliens littering the floor and our carpet. These same picks were being sold in 7-Eleven and Walmart.

A celebrity had called me! Hot Picks were in magazines and thousands of stores. It was a far cry from the garage bands I had friended on MySpace. I am still blown away that a thin piece of plastic could have had such an impact on so many people. It all began with a simple idea.

I believe small, wonderful, simple ideas can be powerful and profitable because I watched my own simple idea explode into a successful business. I watched the lives of the people it touched change. I can think of many other simple ideas that have had an unbelievable effect in the market and on the life of its creator. Remember the Pet Rock? Gary Dahl joked that pets were too messy and that he'd prefer a pet rock, only to go on to sell millions of Pet Rocks. What about Silly Bandz? Elastic wristbands shaped like animals and objects have inspired a global following. Have you heard of iFart? It remains one of the best-selling mobile phone apps. Sara Blakely cut the feet off her pantyhose and created a new clothing staple: Spanx. Ideas such as these have been inspiring me for decades.

Simple ideas are amazing because you can bring them to market yourself. You don't need much. Get ready for an amazing journey!

Acknowledgments

A s anyone who has ever undertaken a major project of any kind knows, there are lots of people to be thanked for their support. I have tried to include everyone here, but of course, I will probably overlook someone and for that I am sorry!

I'd like to start by acknowledging the work that my oldest daughter, Madeleine, did to make this book happen. She listened to hours and hours of audio, which included my ramblings on all the topics in the book. I cannot thank her enough for her patience, all the work she produced, and the coherence that she brought to my thoughts and experiences.

Colleen Sell put my ideas into real words that captured my voice and made my ideas come to life in an easy-to-read manner. Thanks, Colleen.

I want to welcome and thank the newest member of my team, Rhonda Oliver. What a great asset Rhonda is! With her teaching and writing background, she added suggestions and comments that really made the book better. James Shehan, my office and IT manager, is a one-of-a-kind person who has been with me every step of the way. I couldn't run my business without him, and while he knows it, I want to make sure I tell the world here too!

The team at McGraw-Hill has been very supportive and has made it easy to work with their group. Thanks to Mary Glenn, Pamela Peterson, Courtney Fischer, and Pattie Amoroso.

Kirsten Neuhaus, my literary agent, has provided me with great advice whenever I needed it. She's remained calm and professional throughout whatever bumps in the road we've had and I appreciate it!

I also want to thank Gary Krebs for investing the time to help envision the One Simple platform. He helped me look into the future beyond my first book and I am really happy with the vision that I see.

Andrew Krauss has been my business partner for 10 years and I look forward to another 10! He works with our students in such a diligent and helpful way; I really appreciate the hours that he puts in to our shared goals.

My inventRight students and the inventing-entrepreneur community have provided inspiration and support every step of the way. I cannot tell you how fantastic it is to watch students achieve success and bring their dreams to life. It is motivating and rewarding at the same time.

Brian and Bridget Riddle have become lifelong friends and have lived parts of this process with me. I cannot thank them enough for their generosity to my family. Brian, I love you man.

And finally, everyone who has been married for over 20 years knows that you cannot get through these types of projects without the love and support of your family. Jon and Liz, my other two children, have lived through my ups and downs, and miraculously still talk to me. My wife, Janice, has somehow managed to survive all of this with a great sense of humor. She continues to be the love of my life, providing support to me and my children without asking for much in return.

Introduction

I'VE BEEN coming up with simple ideas and bringing them to market for 35 years. For all but a few of those years, I've been my own boss, running my own business. Yet, I'm not an engineer or inventor. I don't have an MBA, and I didn't work my way up the ranks in corporate America. In fact, until recently, when I sold one of my products to a pharmaceutical company and became the head of one of its divisions, I'd worked for someone else only once in my adult life—a three-year stint with a startup company. To fund my own ideas and businesses, I didn't go into debt, bring in investors, get money from family and friends, sell my house, or spend millions of dollars of my own or anybody else's money. In other words, I'm just like most people who have an idea for a product and a dream of starting their own business to bring their idea to market.

I think *everyone* has that dream at one point or another, for one reason or another: You see or use a product that doesn't quite hit the mark and think, *I could do better than that!* Or you can't find something you need or want in stores and think, *Why hasn't someone invented this?* Or you lose your job, or need to make more money, or want more challenge, freedom, and reward from your work—and think, *I should just do my own thing!* Or maybe you're one of those creative people who is always coming up with clever ideas and now you're thinking, *Maybe I can turn my passion into a business!*

Whatever your inspiration or motivation, you come up with an idea for a new product. Then, you start fantasizing about starting a business to bring it to market. You think about how good it will feel to be calling the shots, doing something you really want to do, changing your lifestyle, and maybe even living in a different place. You envision people using your idea, and it makes you feel proud. But you also feel apprehensive. And the more you think about it, mulling over all the unknowns and uncertainties ahead, the more anxious you feel.

So you start questioning yourself: "Is my idea any good? Do I have what it takes? I don't even know what a business plan, balance sheet, branding, and intellectual property are! Am I up for this? Is it the right time? Should I quit my day job? Where do I even start? How much will it cost? What are the risks? What if I bite off more than I can chew? What if I fail?" For most people, that's where the dream ends—in a fantasy extinguished by fear.

I know fear. I've faced it over and over again in my career. So do most entrepreneurs. But over the years I've found ways to reduce the fear—and the risks—of starting a small business and bringing a simple idea to market. I'm going to share those strategies with you in *One Simple Idea for Startups and Entrepreneurs.*

Why I Wrote This Book

I started my first business when I was in my early twenties and knew little about what it takes to be an entrepreneur. At the time, I didn't even know I was an entrepreneur. I just knew I wanted to create and sell my own products. Frankly, I didn't think I had any other skills or way to make a living. So I jumped into the water headfirst—and loved it!

Three decades later, I'm still coming up with simple ideas, although these days I usually leave the marketing, manufacturing, sales, and distribution of my ideas to the companies that license them. Through my company inventRight, I also teach other people how to bring their ideas to market—which is why I wrote my first book, *One Simple Idea: Turn Your Dreams into a Licensing Goldmine While Letting Others Do the Work* (McGraw-Hill, February 2011).

That's also why I've written *One Simple Idea for Startups and Entrepreneurs*: to show people how to bring their ideas to market *themselves*. As I've learned through my own experiences and the experiences of my students and colleagues, licensing isn't for everyone and every idea. Some people want control of everything—developing the product, creating a business, running day-to-day operations, and growing the business over time. Sometimes, the best way, if not the *only* way, to bring an idea to market is to do it all yourself. That was the case nine years ago when I cofounded a small company, Hot Picks, to produce and sell a simple but innovative idea: guitar picks formed like skulls, hearts, and other novelty shapes. Throughout this book, I share the lessons I learned in starting, managing, growing, and ultimately, selling Hot Picks.

A critical lesson I learned early on is that you have to have a product that people want and that generates the income you want. It's not enough for you to love your idea. There has to be a market for it, and you have to be able to bring it to market profitably. Pouring time, money, and resources into an idea that doesn't add up is one of the most common mistakes entrepreneurs make, and it's one of the leading causes of small-business failures. Yet, I've found few books on entrepreneurship, inventing, and small-business ownership that tell you how to do the math to determine whether your idea has merit *before* you go to the time, trouble, and expense of trying to bring it to market.

Another thing lacking from most of the books on this topic that I've read is practical information on how to stay in business and grow your business. According to the United States Small Business Administration, 49 percent of small-business startups fail within five years, 66 percent close their doors within 10 years, and 75 percent are out of business by the 15-year mark. Why so many failures? Why do so few companies stay in business over the long haul? There are many reasons. But I suspect many of these businesses failed because they didn't realize something else I learned early on: it's not enough to bring one idea to market successfully. The market for most products goes up and down, and then either peters out gradually or bottoms out suddenly. For your business to survive and thrive, you have to continually innovate and come out with product ideas that are marketable and profitable.

The magic is in the idea. The means is in the numbers. The rest is just a matter of learning and following the fundamental mechanics of starting and running a business.

I wrote this book to give you the magic and the means as well as the practical tools and know-how to turn your simple idea into a profitable business. *One Simple Idea for Startups and Entrepreneurs* will give you the confidence and competence to jump into the water headfirst. And I'm here to tell you, the water is just fine.

Who This Book Is For

One Simple Idea for Startups and Entrepreneurs is for anyone who has a *simple idea* for a new or improved product and wants (or needs) to start a *small business* to bring it to market themselves, rather than licensing or selling their idea to a big company. It's for people of all ages, all walks of life, and all levels of business experience (or inexperience, as the case may be). And it's for almost every type of product. With my do-it-yourself approach to going into business to develop, produce, and sell your own product idea, you don't need millions of dollars in startup capital and a business, engineering, or manufacturing background. All you need is one simple idea—and the passion to bring it to market.

If your idea is for a complicated product—say, an aerospace, automotive, high-tech, pharmaceutical, or other scientific invention—this book is not for you. Nor is it for people who have an idea for a service-based business. This book is exclusively for people who have ideas for products that are simple to design, make, sell, and distribute.

By the way, those kinds of products account for the lion's share of purchases made by consumers and businesses every year. People buy things like toys, games, tools, sporting goods, office goods, pet goods, household goods, decorative items, novelty items, beauty accessories, gadgets, widgets, and so on much more often than they do things like computers, refrigerators, and cars.

Think of it this way: *One Simple Idea for Startups and Entrepreneurs* isn't so much for the inventor of the wheel as it is for people who reinvent the wheel in clever ways or for new applications . . . and who want to bring their idea to market themselves taking the easiest, safest, fastest route possible. This book shows you that route. It also shows you how to maneuver around potential roadblocks, detours, and shortcuts along the way.

What This Book Is About

One Simple Idea for Startups and Entrepreneurs is a road map that takes you from the starting line (coming up with a great idea) to the finish line (creating a successful business). It gives you the tools, processes, and practical information you need to successfully navigate and execute each leg of the journey: developing, testing, and protecting your idea; planning and launching your business; manufacturing, packaging, marketing, selling, and distributing your product; managing and growing your business; and preparing for and implementing your end game.

First and foremost, this book—like my book on licensing a simple idea—shows you how to pick and design a winning idea so you don't end up with a garage full of stuff you can't sell. It also shows you how to do the math to ensure your idea is profitable, both before you bring it to market as well as throughout the life of your product. Why spend all your time, effort, and hard-earned cash on an idea that nobody wants and will never make you any money?

One Simple Idea for Startups and Entrepreneurs is about starting small and working smart to bring a simple idea to market yourself so that, at the end of the day, you can pay your bills, put money in your pocket, and enjoy your work and your life.

Many of the concepts, strategies, and tips presented in this book are the same or similar to those in my first book, *One Simple Idea: Turn Your Dreams into a Licensing Goldmine*. That's because the fundamentals of finding, developing, and protecting a simple idea are the same whether you license your product to a manufacturer or contract with a manufacturer to bring it to market yourself.

This book is about having the control and independence you want: taking on all the risks and responsibilities, including coming up with the capital to make it happen. It takes you step-by-step through the processes of developing and testing your idea, starting and running your business, marketing and selling your products, and planning and preparing for the company's future. It gives you the information you need to lessen inherent risks, leverage yourself against the big players, get into different retailers, hedge your bets, and much more.

Ultimately, this book answers the questions that put the fear in people's hearts and the kibosh on so many dreams: "Do I have what it takes? Is my idea any good? How do I bring my product to market myself? Can I make a living doing this? Will I be able to build a profitable business I can be proud of and enjoy?"

The answer is: absolutely! . . . when you follow the roadmap to success in *One Simple Idea for Startups and Entrepreneurs*.

Don't let the fear of striking out hold you back.

—Babe Ruth

Opportunities for Inventor-Entrepreneurs in the Twenty-First Century

Tᴴɪꜱ ɪꜱ a fantastic time to be creating new products and bringing them to market yourself!

The opportunities for simple ideas that offer clear benefits to the consumer are endless. Consumer spending accounts for 60 to 70 percent of the U.S. economy, even during economic slumps, and 40 percent of consumer spending is discretionary—driven by desire, not necessity. Dreaming up ideas for consumer products can be a lot of fun. But your simple idea doesn't have to be for a consumer product. It can be for something purchased and used by businesses, governments, scientists, institutions (schools, hospitals, etc.), public service organizations (police, fire, waste management, etc.), and so on.

Even during economic downturns, there are opportunities for innovation. When the economy is poor, the most popular products tend to be those that enable people to stretch their resources (such as squeezing the last bit of toothpaste out of the tube), provide inexpensive comfort or enjoyment, and improve the quality of life without breaking the budget. As I write this, our economic situation is not great, but some markets are strong. For example, the pet and home-improvement industries are both growing by approximately 5 percent a year, and the kitchen industry is on fire because people are staying home to cook.

Regardless of whether the economy is booming or busting, consumers are always open to products that make their lives easier or more enjoyable. You just need to know where to look for them and how to recognize them.

There are also lots of tools and resources available that make it easier than ever to start and grow a business. With the Internet and communication technologies, such as Skype, you can work out of your home rather than locate the business elsewhere. You don't have to sell your product only through brick-and-mortar stores; you can sell it online, too. The Internet enables you to study the market and find most of the information you need. Social media networks allow you to connect with like-minded people who can help you with your business. You can use your website, blogs, social media networks, e-mail, and other online tools to build your brand and communicate with customers and vendors.

All these tools make it easier for anyone to compete in the big leagues. You can get closer to and be more responsive to the market. You can bring products to market faster, seizing market opportunities the heavy hitters miss or don't want to bother with. You can provide a level of personalized customer service that most large companies don't care to do.

All of these things can be done from your desk, with just your telephone and computer—no fancy office or employees needed. Everything can be outsourced, from creating a technical drawing of your idea to manufacturing your product, designing your logo, and doing your bookkeeping! You can tap into creative ways to fund your business, too.

All the information, resources, and tools you need to successfully launch a small business and bring a simple idea to market yourself are out there. You just need a road map to show you how to find them, use them, and get from here to there. That's what this book is all about.

My Journey

During the 35 years I've been bringing simple ideas to market, I've done more than just license my products. I've also worked for a startup company where I helped bring other people's ideas to market, and I've started a business to bring my own ideas to market—not once, but twice. In fact, that's how I began this journey, so let's start at the beginning.

In the mid-1970s, I was a freshman at Santa Clara University majoring in economics and hating everything about it. I felt overwhelmed and needed to try something different. So I took an art class and fell in love with working with my hands. One day, I went home and told my dad I wanted to be an artist.

"That's fantastic, Steve!" he said. "Do you draw?"

"No."

"Do you paint?"

"No."

Dad sighed and studied me for a long minute. Then, he said, "Find your passion, Steve. Then do it, and you'll never work a day in your life." It was the best advice he ever gave me.

I transferred to San Jose State University because it had a huge art department, and I changed my major to art. That wasn't the right fit for me, either, because I was creative but not a fine artist. When I left college three years later, I didn't know what I was going to do. I didn't think I had the skills to get a job. I had to find a way to earn a living, so I started to make things.

I made t-shirts with funny sayings on them and ran advertisements in the back of national magazines to try to sell them, but I didn't have much luck. I added funny hats with adjustable fingers in the back that you could bend into a peace sign, okay sign, or other symbols, but I didn't have much luck selling them either. I didn't give up, though, and began making soft sculptures (stuffed animals and characters). I would come up with ideas, source the materials from local fabric stores, handmake the products, and sell them at arts and crafts fairs up and down the state of California.

I'll never forget my first show. It was a small art-and-crafts festival in the Santa Cruz Mountains. It seemed like a big deal to me at the time, but it was actually just a bunch of tables and handmade booths set up in the playground of an elementary school. I was sitting there at my little table covered with my Softies when my dad showed up.

"How're you doing?" he asked.

"Fantastic!"

"Good!" he said. "How many products have you sold?"

I hadn't sold any. But I loved it, stayed with it, and learned from it. One of the best lessons I learned very quickly was that if I was going to eat and pay my rent, I had to come up with ideas people loved. If a product didn't sell, I had to immediately replace it with one that did. The experience taught me to be agile: quick to realize and respond to what customers did and didn't like. I spent about six years designing, making, and selling my stuff at street fairs, loving every aspect of that little world.

Unfortunately, everyone (and I mean *everyone*) thought I was a loser. I could see the question in their faces: What are you doing with your life? You're 25 and selling things on the street? Besides, I wanted more for myself and my ideas. I thought, *If I can sell my little products at street fairs, why not in local stores? And if I can sell my products in local stores, why not in big stores all over the country? Why not all over the world?* I wanted to see my products everywhere!

One day, I loaded up my partner Marlena's Mustang with a crate of our products, a series of soft-sculpture vegetables with smiling faces we'd made out of colored nylons we purchased at a local department store. I drove to downtown Los Gatos, where there were a lot of novelty stores. I found one that seemed perfect: Puttin' on the Ritz. The owner, Marilyn Hart, was very kind. She treated me with respect, even though I didn't have a clue what I was doing, and she let me show her my products, even though they weren't right for her store. Then she gave me a mini-lesson in retail pricing—explaining how a store would *keystone* my product (mark it up)—and some other advice before sending me on my way, without an order but inspired to keep trying.

Two more stores turned me down, and although I was discouraged, it wasn't enough to make me stop. I went to the Rainbow Inn at the Pacific Garden Mall in Santa Cruz, a store I had frequented as a customer and knew had a lot of soft sculpture. I hauled in my crate and was trying, unsuccessfully, to convince the manager to carry my product when a woman walked up to the register to make a purchase. "What's that?" she asked me. I pulled out a Softie to show her; she loved it and bought it on the spot. Right then and there, the store owner said he wanted to carry a dozen Softies. That was my first—and only—retail order! But it was enough to convince me I could get into retail.

A couple months later, I opened my own retail store. On one side of the shop, we sold the Softies we made; on the other side, we sold plants and jewelry. On opening day we sold enough to pay the first month's rent. During the three years I had the store, I continued to sell my products at local street fairs. I also still wanted to get them into other stores. I just didn't know how. But I would soon find out.

• • •

It was Labor Day weekend, and I was at the Sausalito Art Festival in the San Francisco Bay Area. A man came up to my booth and asked whether my products were available in stores.

"Only at my own shop in Santa Cruz," I said.

"You need to contact Steve Askin," he said. "He can get your stuff into stores everywhere." Then he told me about Steve, the "Gizmo King," inventor of Deely Bobbers (headbands with pom-pom antennae sticking up from them, inspired by the "Killer Bees" costumes on *Saturday Night Live*), and his company, What's New, which represented artists and designers from all over the United States.

I happened to call Steve when he was in the midst of setting up a trade show where retail buyers from around the country would come to select merchandise for their stores. Mistaking me for someone else, he told me to bring in my stuff. I asked my father to come along, because I was still wet behind the ears and figured that he, a lifelong manager at General Electric, had a lot more business experience than I did. The showroom was filled with antique toys, dancing stuffed animals, and a riot of novelty items. We sat across from Steve Askin in chairs molded like a ballerina and a basketball player; he was wearing a Hawaiian shirt and a Deely Bobber with money-sign antennae on his head. Dad felt like he'd landed on Mars, and I felt right at home!

Steve fell in love with my products. If I could make them, he would sell them. I assured him I could, and he immediately put them on display in his showroom. Sure enough, the orders started flowing in. But I wasn't prepared for the volume; I was making everything by hand and couldn't keep up. With the interest in the product and its price point, I needed to find a cost-effective and less labor-intensive way to make them. Steve had a manufacturing facility in the garment district at the time, and he showed me how he manufactured his products. I taught his group how to make my designs, and they were able to make them faster and at a better price, even though they were still handmade.

So Steve took over manufacturing while I focused on designing more Softies, and we divvied up the profits. It was my first experience with manufacturing. In hindsight, it was my first experience with licensing, too. Steve was also the first person to tell me I wasn't crazy and could actually make a living doing this, and he's continued to be my mentor over the years.

• • •

Although my products were selling well through What's New, I wanted to get them into more and bigger stores, especially big-box retailers such as Target and Walmart. By then, I realized that to get my products out to the mass market I had to find a faster, cheaper way to manufacture them.

I was fortunate to meet a woman who was fascinated with my creations and pointed me in the direction of patternmaking. Patterns could be sewn by a workforce and made quickly. So I spent the summer learning how to make patterns.

Soon after, I visited Dakin, the largest manufacturer of plush stuffed animals in the United States at the time. The day I chose to go to Dakin proved to be fortuitous: their lead designer had just quit. The timing couldn't have been better. People there sent me home with an assignment to make a life-size plush golden retriever and told me to come back in two weeks. If they liked it, they would pay me $1,500. When I cashed that check, I felt like a million bucks! That was my first freelance job designing a product for a mass-market retailer.

A few months after that, I read an article about a teddy bear from a new company called Worlds of Wonder (WOW), in Fremont, California. The bear (Teddy Ruxpin) talked and moved its mouth, but it was pretty ugly to me. I thought I could do better, so I contacted WOW and offered to design a cuter bear for the company on a freelance basis. Instead, WOW hired me. They were planning to manufacture a line of electronic plush toys and needed a designer to create patterns and oversee manufacturing. I was in my late twenties and had my first real job.

The company sent me overseas to supervise manufacturing, and I worked with packaging designers and contractors. I went to trade shows and sat in on meetings where the major players at WOW discussed why an idea was good or bad. I also did a lot of design work for WOW, and eventually was promoted to manager of design and even had a few people working under me. I learned about every facet of bringing a product to market in a corporate environment and for a worldwide mass market. What I learned and experienced there changed my life. WOW sold more than five million Teddy Ruxpins in the first year at $89 a pop and became the fifth largest toy company in the world—with only one product. The best part of being at WOW was that I met my beautiful wife, Janice, there. The most important thing I learned was that the guy who created Teddy Ruxpin and licensed it to WOW made more than a million dollars a month in royalties!

That really got my attention. Licensing appealed to me because it would enable me to focus on what I loved and did best: being creative. Plus, I was fearful that I still didn't have the skills, knowledge, or desire to start and run my own company, and licensing felt like a safer way to bring my simple ideas to market. So I left WOW and started my own product design company, Stephen Key Design, LLC.

• • •

In the beginning, I was the CEO, president, sole designer, and single employee of Stephen Key Design. I got off to a good start because I was able to submit my ideas to the manufacturing companies for which

I had done consultant work at WOW. I also did some freelance product design work for those and other manufacturers. Companies such as Applause licensed my ideas, and that took me to the next level—seeing my own product ideas on the shelves of mass market retailers. Ohio Art licensed a basketball game from me that sold for more than 10 years, and Trudeau licensed my cup and canteen ideas, which sold well in Disney stores and theme parks for many years.

Over the years, I've licensed more than 20 ideas to companies in many industries. When I was in my forties, after reading that there wasn't enough space on labels to provide all the important information consumers needed to know about products they were consuming or using, I came up with the idea for a "spinning" label that wrapped around the container. The opportunities in the labeling industry were huge, and my Spinformation® label turned out to be the best-selling idea of my career (so far).

But things change. They *always* change. Royalties from the Spinformation label stopped. The label was too expensive to manufacture. I was also tired of the daily grind and needed a change; I wanted to do something new.

• • •

That's when Rob Stephani, a friend from my childhood, walked back into my life. We both knew a guy who was making a lot of money selling a guitar pick with the image of an alien head printed on it. Later, I kept thinking about that guitar pick and playing around with ideas for guitar pick designs. Then it hit me: rather than just printing an image on the surface, why not change the shape of the pick, too? As long as the picks were the standard sizes and thicknesses and in the basic shape of a rounded triangle, why couldn't they be shaped like skulls or monsters?

We had some skull picks made and took them to the largest music trade show in America, where we gave away the Grave Picker, as we called it. Our booth was packed. I knew then and there we had a hit.

I also knew from my research that the two companies dominating the market would never license my idea. But we knew it would sell.

Rob had a music store for 15 years, so he knew all the distributors. We figured the picks would cost only pennies to make. I could design the picks, Rob could sell them, and a local contract manufacturer could make them. How hard could it be?

Well, it was harder than I'd thought. But we did it, and it was extremely rewarding to see all of our hard work come to fruition. Hot Picks ended up in tens of thousands of stores worldwide—including major chains such as Walmart and 7-Eleven. Once again, my products were in mass market retailers! This time, I'd brought them to market myself. In a way, I'd come full circle, like when I was in my twenties making and selling my Softies—but on a larger scale. This time, I was manufacturing rather than handmaking my products, and I was selling my products nationwide through retailers rather than handselling at local street fairs or in my little brick-and-mortar store.

I had a blast! I got to work with some great bands and great people, such as Taylor Swift and her family. I had complete control. And I learned a tremendous amount about starting and running a business to bring my own ideas to market—all of which I'm going to share with you in this book.

Successful Inventor-Entrepreneurs in This Book

I asked several inventor-entrepreneurs from a variety of industries to share their experiences, knowledge, and advice with us in this book. You'll hear from them throughout these pages. Let me introduce them now.

Amy Baxter, M.D.
Founder/Owner/CEO of MMJ Labs
Simple idea: Buzzy®
http://www.buzzy4shots.com

Dr. Amy Baxter is a pediatric emergency physician, pain researcher, and busy mother of three children under the age of 15. In 2006, she started her company, MMJ Labs, to bring her idea—a simple medical device that relieves the minor pain of injections and needle pricks—to market.

The company's founding product, Buzzy, is a palm-sized, plastic, vibrating "bee" whose "wings" are cold packs. The combination of gentle vibration and cold confuses the body's nerves, distracting the brain's attention away from the sharp pain of shots and from stinging, burning, itching, and prickling sensations. Buzzy dulls or eliminates the pain of injections and needle pricks by sending the vibrating and cooling sensations along the same nerves the pain is traveling, much like rubbing a bumped elbow or running cool water over a burn does.

Since Buzzy was launched in May 2009, it has been adopted by more than 100 hospitals and more than 5,000 users. Originally designed for children, Buzzy is now also available in a plain black unit (without the charming bee image and shape). The company also markets other related products, including a line of Bee-Stractor™ cards and posters that reduce pain by distracting pediatric patients.

Annette Giacomazzi
Founder/Owner of MediFAB3
Simple idea: CastCoverZ®
http://www.castcoverz.com

In her "previous life," Annette Giacomazzi was a high-level sales executive selling to Fortune 500 CEOs. Then came marriage, two children, a vineyard that gave way to an olive ranch and, in 2008, a simple idea that led her to launch her own business: producing fun, fashionable, durable, washable cloth covers for orthopedic casts. The first CastCoverZ, as she named them, was a line of covers for arm casts. But then, during the process of developing the product and starting the business, Annette was diagnosed with breast cancer. After a year-long hiatus to treat and recover from the cancer, she came back swinging.

Three years after coming up with her simple idea, CastCoverZ was open for business! Today, there are 10 different CastCoverZ product lines—for orthopedic casts, boots, splints, braces, slings, and wraps.

Each line is available in different sizes and in numerous fabric choices. Today, CastCoverZ is the leading brand of cast covers in the United States, sold in prominent orthopedic clinics and children's hospitals across the country. The company also has European distribution and now sells five lines of companion products.

Leslie Haywood
Founder/Owner/President of Charmed Life Products, LLC
Simple idea: Grill Charms™
http://www.grillcharms.com

After receiving a bachelor's degree in organizational communications in 1993, Leslie Haywood enjoyed a nine-year career in the import/export industry, climbing the ranks to customer service manager. When her first daughter was born in 2002, she "left a fantastic company and wonderful career to be a stay-at-home mom." Her second daughter was born in 2004, and Leslie had no plans to return to work for a long time.

Then, in April 2006, she came up with the idea for Grill Charms: doodads, similar in concept to wine charms, that make it easy for whoever is cooking and whoever is eating food cooked on a grill or broiler to easily distinguish different steak temperatures, spices, and flavors, and health or allergy factors. The dime-sized, stainless steel charms have a decorative coin-shaped head with the identifying emblem stamped into the metal (for example, "Rare" or "Spicy") and a serrated stem to secure the charm in the food while it is cooking and served.

In June 2006, while in the midst of developing her product idea, Leslie was diagnosed with breast cancer. In August 2006, she had a bilateral mastectomy, and in the fall of that year, she launched her business, Charmed Life Products. In November 2007, her first packaged collection, The Steak Collection, was released. The company now has three additional packaged collections, The Spicy Collection, The Charmed Life Collection, and The Pink Collection. Grill Charms are sold online and in retail stores throughout the United States.

Linda Jangula
Founder/Owner/Manager of Jalyn Enterprise, LLC
Simple idea: Wiki Wags®
http://www.mywikiwags.com

Linda Jangula began training dogs for competition showing when she was a young child, and she has been an American Kennel Club (AKC) dog breeder for more than 30 years. In January 2011, she invented a new and improved disposable diaper for male dogs. Wiki Wags are like a cummerbund that wraps around the dog's abdomen, covering the genitals with an absorbent, urine-wicking shield to prevent the dog from spraying or marking its territory while indoors. The shield also wicks the urine away from the dog's body, keeping the animal dry and comfortable. Wiki Wags come in four different sizes.

In June 2011, Linda launched her company and brought her simple idea to market. Wiki Wags are available online and in numerous retail stores throughout the United States.

David Mayer
Founder/Owner of Clean Bottle
Simple idea: Clean Bottle
http://www.cleanbottle.com

David Mayer is a Stanford University graduate, Ironman triathlete, former Silicon Valley product line manager, and avid cycler. In 2007, he conceived of a new type of sports bottle that has a cap on both ends and a removable drinking spout for easier, more sanitary cleaning. Three years later, in May 2010, the first Clean Bottle product was launched. The Original, as it is called, is made of BPA-free, nontoxic plastic, and it is recyclable, freezable, and dishwasher safe.

Clean Bottles can be found in more than 4,000 retail stores and major distributors throughout the United States and Europe, including REI, Performance Bicycle, Dick's Sporting Goods, Sport Chalet, GNC, and 24 Hour Fitness, as well as independent bicycle shops. In early 2012, the company launched The Runner, the first (and only, so far) sports-bottle holder that allows the runner to easily access his/her iPod or smart phone while running, hiking, or walking and without fiddling with the holder. In the summer of 2012, The Square, a stainless steel version of the Clean Bottle, made its debut.

Nancy Tedeschi
Founder/Owner of Eyeego, LLC
Simple idea: SnapIt®
http://www.snapitscrew.com

While running a title company, which she owned for 20 years, Nancy Tedeschi started a small business to bring her simple idea—decorative eyeglass charms—to market herself. Six years later, in 2010, she changed the name of the company to Eyeego and launched another invention, SnapIt screws. The SnapIt is a tiny, stainless steel screw with a feeder tab that enables the optical technician or eyeglass wearer to easily guide the screw into the threaded hole of the eyeglass frame or hinge. The tab is then snapped off and discarded.

The large distributor of SnapIt screws, OptiSource, sold more than 2.3 million units in the first 12 months of its contract with Eyeego. SnapIt screws are now being sold in some European markets and in retail stores throughout the United States, including Ace Hardware, Bartell Drugs, Bi-Mart, Giant Eagle, Office Depot, Rite Aid, True Value, and Walgreens.

Craig Wolfe
Founder/Owner/President of CelebriDucks
Simple idea: CelebriDucks
http://www.celebriducks.com

CelebriDucks began as an offshoot of Craig Wolfe's original company, Name That Toon, which developed and sold the first animation art lines for Coca-Cola, Anheuser-Busch, M&M/Mars, Pillsbury, Campbell Soup, Hershey, and other major brands. Name That Toon grew to become the largest publisher of advertising/animation art in the country.

In 1998, Craig and his team started developing the CelebriDucks as a "little fun side project." CelebriDucks are collectible rubber ducks made in the images of iconic figures in film, music, athletics, and history. The company has produced CelebriDucks for the National Basketball Association, Major League Baseball, the National Hockey League, and the National Association for Stock Car Auto Racing (NASCAR). Celebrity ducks include Betty Boop, Groucho Marx, the Three Stooges, KISS, James Brown, the Blues Brothers, Charlie Chaplin, Mr. T, Shakespeare, and Barack Obama. The company has created more than 200 CelebriDucks to date, and the brand continues to evolve as new editions are introduced and others are "retired to the pond."

CelebriDucks are sold around the world. In 2012, the company introduced a new line of CelebriDucks gift sets in which a collectible rubber duck is packaged with a box of Canard (French for "duck") chocolate or handmade soap.

IF I COULD GO BACK AND START UP AGAIN
Nancy Tedeschi/SnapIt

I've been an entrepreneur since 1990, when I started my own mortgage title company. But when I launched a business to bring my eyeglass charms and then my Snap-It screws to market, I entered a whole new world. It's a scary, lonely process. For the first few years, I freaked out daily and spent a lot of nights lying awake wondering, *Oh, my God! What if this doesn't work?* I made a lot of mistakes, but I always found a way. When you're in that zone, when you've invested all your time and money, it's like having a baby. You have to be patient and persistent.

It's turned out better than I could have imagined, to the point that I sometimes feel like I'm having an out-of-body experience! So I don't have any regrets. But if I could go back and do it over again, I would definitely have sat down with somebody who had already done what I was trying to do and asked them a lot of questions. I'd have found a mentor who had a successful business and products on the shelf, and I'd have picked his or her brains.

Finding a Mentor

One of the best things you can do for yourself and your business is to find someone who has more experience and knowledge than you do to mentor you. Ideally, your mentor will be an inventor-entrepreneur who has successfully brought to market at least one product similar to yours or in the same industry. You want someone with whom you can build a rapport and who will not only teach but also encourage you.

I've had many mentors throughout my career. In my experience, people who are older tend to be more willing to offer their time and share their knowledge. So I usually seek out mature entrepreneurs with years of experience and lots of success under their belts. But many younger inventor-entrepreneurs have much to share and are willing to help.

So how do you go about finding a mentor? I'd start local, in your own hometown. One of the companies in our small town, 511 Tactical, was doing extremely well and always being written up in the newspaper. I knew someone who worked there, so I called him and said, "Hey, I started this company and I'm having some trouble controlling inventory. Can you help me or maybe give me a tour and show me a few things?" He showed me his whole operation, and I got to see how the company had solved its inventory problems. As time went on, we became friends, and I knew I could always call on him for advice and information.

Another good place to meet entrepreneurs is the local Rotary Club; members are often successful people who want to give back to the community. You could try your local Small Business Administration (SBA) chapter; that organization has a wide network of local people. Read articles and blogs written by successful inventor-entrepreneurs or experts in whatever area in which you need help. Just contact the author and begin the dialogue by commenting on his or her article or blog. If that person can't help you, he or she may be able to recommend someone who can. If a successful entrepreneur or industry expert is teaching a class at your local college, you could sit in on a class and make a connection that way. The online social network LinkedIn (http:///www.linkedin.com) is a great place to find a senior member of a company or a retiree willing to give you some advice. You might find a mentor through a trade association or at a trade show or other industry meet-up.

When you find people you're interested in connecting with, don't start out by asking for help. You don't want them to feel pressured or put upon. Show an interest in them first. When I meet or hear about people whose backgrounds interest me, I'm curious about their success, so I reach out to them and ask about their products, their companies, their stories. They sense I'm genuinely interested, which opens the door. Most people love to talk about themselves and sincerely want to help others. At the end of the day, you want them to feel good about helping you and being a part of your success.

2

Do You Have What It Takes?

So you've come up with a simple idea for a new product, and you want to start a business to bring it to market yourself. But you've never done this before, and the road ahead looks a little scary and more than a little risky. So you're starting to question yourself.

It's not as ominous as it seems, and it's not uncharted territory. Others have gone before you, and you can learn much from their experiences, which is what this book is about. But only you can answer the do-or-don't question that preys on the mind of virtually every person who's embarked on this journey: *do I have what it takes?*

That question certainly weighed on my mind when we started Hot Picks. I definitely didn't have all the traits experts say it takes to start a business and make it successful. And I had a lot of self-doubt.

We all have self-doubt. We all lack some of the key attributes of a successful entrepreneur. But credentials and confidence alone don't a successful entrepreneur make, because the most essential component of success is the product itself. If the idea stinks, the business will sink. The magic is in the idea. Everything else can be learned.

Entrepreneur: Born or Made?

Some people claim that you're either born with the traits and abilities associated with being a successful entrepreneur or you're not. Others claim that virtually anyone can develop the traits and abilities necessary for entrepreneurial success.

I've been an entrepreneur for a long time, and I've known and worked with a lot of them. Here's what I think: Some traits associated with entrepreneurial success come naturally to some people, but most people can develop most of those traits if they want to. And no one needs to have them all in order to turn a simple idea into a successful business.

In my observation and opinion, these are the top 10 traits of successful entrepreneurs:

1. **Passionate**. The most important trait an entrepreneur can have is passion: for your idea, your customers, your business, and your work. When you're passionate about something, it is so interesting and meaningful to you that it's all you want to do, and you want to share it with everyone. Passion drives you to do more and be better, to overcome the tough times, and to achieve your goals.

2. **Independent**. Most successful entrepreneurs relish their independence and love to be in charge. They have a strong desire to be their own boss and a strong aversion to working for someone else. Having this sense of self-determination empowers you to take initiative and responsibility. It also helps you be decisive and resourceful.

3. **Creative**. Successful entrepreneurs have the ability to "think outside the box"; to ask "what if" and then envision it; to see connections, opportunities, and solutions other people miss. Being an entrepreneur is all about being unique—in designing your products, marketing your brand, solving problems, and running your business.

4. **Optimistic**. Successful entrepreneurs believe in their ideas and in themselves. They tend to have a positive outlook, trusting they will find whatever answers, resources, and opportunities they need to succeed. Having confidence in yourself gives your customers, vendors, and employees more confidence in you. Having a positive outlook helps you make good decisions, take constructive action, and seek solutions to challenges.

5. **Willing to take risks and action**. Successful entrepreneurs take calculated risks and purposeful action. They have the ability to recognize and assess opportunities as well as risks. But what really gives them the edge is their gumption to go for it. You can learn how to identify, assess, and reduce your risks. You can learn how to find, generate, and assess opportunities. You can learn how to devise a great action plan. But you have to be willing to take risks and action. Opportunities don't wait, and sometimes the only way to get where you want to be is to take a leap of faith.

6. **Open-minded**. At a talk on entrepreneurship I attended, the speaker said, "You have to be able to live with the unknown." That's so true. Successful entrepreneurs are open-minded, flexible, and able to learn and adapt as they go. You're never going to have all the answers; in fact, you're going to have to make educated guesses half the time. So you have to be comfortable with ambiguity, open to opportunities, and willing to learn and adapt as you go.

7. **Good networker**. Although successful entrepreneurs are self-directed, they love to network. They constantly look for ways to connect with people and to leverage those connections. They are not afraid to ask questions or seek help. Having good networking skills will enable you to surround yourself with people who are willing and able to lend their support. It will also help you build strong relationships with customers and vendors.

8. **Resilient**. All successful entrepreneurs have failed and made mistakes, but they have the ability to learn and recover from their mistakes and failures. Because they are oriented toward goals and solutions, they look for ways to avoid and resolve problems, and they don't give up easily. Starting small and with a simple idea reduces your risks and enables you to respond to problems more quickly and effectively. But you're going to make mistakes and have setbacks. So you have to be willing and able to get through them and grow from them.

9. **Persistent**. Successful entrepreneurs understand that bringing an idea to market and building a business take a lot of hard work,

and they are willing to put in the time and work to achieve their goals. They are tenacious problem solvers who approach obstacles as stepping-stones, rather than as barriers to success, and they never just take no for an answer. If one strategy doesn't work, they keep trying different ones until they get the results they are after or exhaust every viable tactic. Passion fires you up; persistence enables you to go the distance.

10. **Driven**. All successful entrepreneurs are driven to succeed. I also think many are driven by a purpose that is personal and meaningful to them. It may be the desire to make a lot of money or a positive difference in the world. It may be the need to prove something to yourself or others. It may be the longing to transform yourself or simply to do something you love. When you know what you want and go for it, you are more likely to get it.

Of course, having these 10 traits doesn't necessarily guarantee success. In fact, some of these characteristics can be problematic. If you're too independent, for example, you may think your way is the only one and may not take input from others. If you take persistence too far, you may pour time, effort, and money into a lost cause.

I know I don't have all the right traits, and there are many parts of being an entrepreneur that still scare me, such as the unknowns and the risks. But I think most, if not all, of these qualities can be learned. So if you have some of these traits and the willingness to develop the others, you have what it takes to be a successful inventor-entrepreneur. The question is: is it what you want?

Does the Shoe Fit?

Just because you have the right traits to be a successful entrepreneur does not mean it's the right thing for you. Maybe, for personal or health reasons, you're not up to it. Maybe you have other priorities that take precedence. Maybe the timing isn't right. As you will learn in this book, there are ways to minimize the fears and risks of bringing your product to market yourself—first and foremost, by starting small and with a simple idea. But it also helps to understand what you are getting into and whether it's right for you *before* you take the leap.

To help you decide whether you want to take one route rather than another, such as licensing or selling your idea to a company, let's take a look at a few realities facing inventor-entrepreneurs and some correlating questions you should ask yourself.

Reality: You're Going to Be the Top Dog, and It Can Get Hairy, Scary, and Lonely Up There

I love the creativity, control, and freedom of being an entrepreneur. But with freedom comes responsibility: 100 percent responsibility for every decision, action, problem, mistake, and facet of your business.

To help you decide whether you want to be the boss, ask yourself the following questions:

"Do I have a burning desire to be in charge?" I've never wanted to work for someone else, but my passion is being the chief *innovation* officer, not the chief *executive* officer. Frankly, being in charge of a whole business is kind of intimidating to me. But I got past that by talking with people who had done it before and finding simpler ways to do things. It also helped to have a partner with expertise in some areas I wasn't comfortable and experienced with.

"Am I a strong leader, willing and able to motivate and manage people?" I'm not a born leader, but I'm trying to learn to be a good leader. What I am good at is working with people and picking good people to work with, which, I've learned, is half of what it takes to be a strong leader.

"Do I embrace and adapt to change?" I can change if I have to, but it's not always easy for me. I don't jump on something simply because it's the latest thing. I weigh the pros and cons of making a change in my product or business, and proceed (or not) based on that assessment.

"Am I self-confident and self-directed?" I really don't need a boss, and my confidence has grown over time and with experience. But sometimes I do need direction or would like a second option. Then, I have no problem asking one of my mentors or some other knowledgeable person for advice or information.

"Do I perform well under pressure and seek solutions to problems?" I freak out under pressure. When that happens, I give myself 24 hours to calm down and remind myself that I'll never have all the answers. (No one ever does.) Then I try to solve the problem by listening, learning, and looking at it from different perspectives.

"Can I make tough decisions and take timely action?" I tend to make decisions too fast, and sometimes they are wrong. I've had to learn to slow down and think about things first. I've also found that I make better choices when I do the research and do the math as part of the process. The other thing I've learned is that most mistakes can be corrected.

Reality: You're Going to Work Harder Than You've Ever Worked in Your Life

Being an entrepreneur involves a huge amount of work, dedication, and sacrifice. If you enjoy working from 9 to 5, following the same routine day in and day out, and having plenty of paid time off, you probably shouldn't start your own business. Because owning your own business means you're going to have to wear many hats, juggle many projects at the same time, deal with constant surprises and crises, and work a lot more than 40 hours a week, at least for the first few years.

To help you decide whether you really want to work that hard, ask yourself these questions:

"Can I work long hours, with little or no time off, for extended periods of time?" I love what I'm doing and I'm healthy, so I work a lot, sometimes to the detriment of my family and friends. Balance is one of the things I continue to work on. Meanwhile, the strategies I've developed to simplify the process of bringing a product to market have made my job (and will make yours) a lot easier and less time-consuming.

"Am I willing and able to wear many hats?" At the beginning, I was not even aware I needed to do so many different things. I have learned to embrace the different hats I must wear, and I've found ways to get things done easily and cheaply, including outsourcing things I'm not good at and don't enjoy.

"Can I handle multiple responsibilities at the same time?" I can deal with having many responsibilities, but I cannot multitask at all. Fortunately, with my step-by-step process for bringing a simple idea to market, I (and you) don't have to juggle several balls at once and risk dropping one or more of them.

"Do I enjoy learning and doing new things?" I like learning new things, and I'm open to try new things. My hands might get sweaty, but I work through it because I realize how important it is. Having mentors and a road map definitely help to relieve the anxiety, too.

"Can I shift gears and reprioritize?" This is one area in which my attention deficit disorder actually helps me. I can switch from one task or project to another very quickly and then go back to what I was doing later. With the ADD, I can't focus on one thing for too long, anyway, so having to shift gears feels natural, rather than disruptive, to me. Having a step-by-step road map to follow helps keep me on track, too.

Reality: It's Going to Take Time and Money, Possibly More Than You Think

I've learned ways to cut the time and cost of bringing a product to market. I've also discovered methods of doing my homework and figuring the math so I can more accurately predict the resources, time, and money I'll actually need. And I share those techniques throughout this book.

But I've also learned two other things: (1) Even with starting small and keeping it simple, it always takes longer and costs more than expected. (2) The bigger you become, the more money it takes to keep going and to grow. So you need to plan and prepare for both of those probabilities, which you'll learn how to do in this book.

To help you decide whether you want to pour all your time and money into your business, ask yourself these questions:

"Do I have the money and other resources I'll need?" Very few inventor-entrepreneurs have all the funding they'll need. One of the advantages of starting small and with a simple idea is that it usually means lower startup costs. There are ways to raise some money, which you'll learn about later in this book.

"Am I comfortable with unknowns and risks?" I hate the unknown and surprises! I like to know where I'm going before I get there. As uncomfortable as I am with risk, it's amazing I am an entrepreneur. I have learned how to overcome that discomfort and to reduce risks, and you'll find out how to do the same.

"Can I wait for success and profitability?" I'm probably the most impatient person you'll ever meet, but I've learned to be more patient, and I've always been persistent. I've also discovered ways to reduce the time it takes to bring a product to market, the most important of which is to start with a simple idea.

Reality: You're Going to Have to Constantly Sell, Sell, Sell!

If you build it, they will *not* just come. And by "they," I don't mean just customers. And by "it," I don't mean just your product. To succeed, you're going to have to sell your idea, your company, and yourself to everyone who has anything to do with your business: vendors, investors, partners, patent examiners, lawyers, employees, manufacturing representatives, distributors, wholesalers, retailers, consumers, the media, industry watchdogs, regulators, and so on. You're going to have to make cold calls, talk with strangers, and build relationships. So you have to believe in yourself and what you're doing, and turn a lot of other people into believers, too.

To help you decide whether you want to be a relentless salesperson for your business, ask yourself these questions:

"Am I crazy in love with my idea?" I have to be in love with my idea. I don't chase the money. Remember, money will follow if you love what you do and you're excited about your product.

"Am I confident in myself and driven to succeed?" Although I'm confident about some of my abilities, I'm not a very confident person overall. But I do want to succeed, perhaps because of my lack of self-confidence. One thing that bolsters my confidence is knowledge, so I'm always trying to learn. I've found that one of the best ways to learn is from someone who has done it before. Pushing past the fear and just doing it also builds confidence. Experience has taught me that if I mess up, I'll learn something from it and get past it.

"Do I enjoy talking about my idea and my experiences?" This is one quality I have in spades. You can't shut me up. Fortunately, I've learned how to use my gift of gab to get vendors, stores, customers, and other people almost as excited about my products as I am. I've also learned when and how to reign it in.

"Am I willing and able to approach strangers and initiate conversations?" A long time ago, I realized that most people are more insecure than I am and more receptive than you might think. Everybody is just trying to do their jobs. Stores are simply trying to make their shoppers happy. Creating a product people want to buy is a win-win proposition for everybody. If you can communicate the unique benefit your product offers, trust me, others will want to hear about it and be glad you took the initiative to bring it to their attention.

"Can I interact with all kinds of people, including those who have a different viewpoint from me or are difficult to deal with?" I have difficulty with other people's opinions and with being part of a team of which I'm not the leader; these can be good traits for an inventor-entrepreneur, but they can also backfire. I'd rather not deal at all with unpleasant people, and, in certain situations, it's my way or the highway. But, I realize the value of establishing and maintaining good working relationships with customers, vendors, business partners, and employees. The key to that, I've learned, is being willing and able to listen and learn. When I understand, I communicate and problem-solve more effectively.

"Do I ask for what I want and persist until I get it or exhaust every option and opportunity?" To a large extent, this comes back to passion. If I believe in my product and what I'm doing, I'll keep asking and working every angle I can think of to get the information, cooperation, order, or whatever I'm after. But I've also learned when to back off, regroup, try again, or let go.

So did you answer yes to all or most of those questions? Or were your answers more like mine: absolutely yes on a few and varying degrees of yes, maybe, and no on the others? You don't have to be perfectly suited for this journey in order to succeed. I'm a serial entrepreneur; I've been doing this for about 30 years, and I'm still not comfortable with all of it. But, then, if you start small and with a simple idea, you don't have to be comfortable at first with all the realities you'll face and confident in your ability to deal with all of them. As you'll learn throughout this book, there are ways to get more comfortable, confident, and competent.

The most important thing is passion. With me, once I found something I really loved, the rest was easy. You, too, have to be so passionate about your idea that you want to share it with everyone and do everything you can to make it happen.

LOOK FOR THE UPSIDE OF A DOWNFALL
Annette Giacomazzi/CastCoverZ

When I made my very first product, I had to order a minimum of 600 units from my manufacturing contractor, and it was a huge, scary thing. I had to provide a "marked" and "graded" computer-generated pattern. I didn't even know what the manufacturer was talking about. Luckily, he referred me to a pattern maker who took my silly little pattern and created a marked and graded digital version of it.

I also had to supply the manufacturer in San Diego with the fabric and elastic. Fortunately, I'd gone through that learning curve during the prototype stage. So I picked out a bright, cheerful fabric and sent it to the West Coast. After the first run was finished, the arm covers were sent to me, and I started selling and shipping them to doctor's offices, orthopedic clinics, and hospitals.

One day I received a phone call from a nurse. "Is this a latex-free product?" she asked.

I paused for a panic-filled moment, not knowing the answer. Then I said, "I'll get back to you shortly."

Well, the elastic used in the product at the time was latex, and some people are allergic or sensitive to latex. So I had to pull 550 units off the shelf and start all over again. But I took a deep breath and a step back, and tried to figure out what to do with all those unsellable products. That's when it hit me: *Those are samples! I invested in 550 samples!*

Mistakes happen. Just accept that, find something positive about it, and move on. Then it won't be that hairy, scary monster lurking in the corner anymore.

Startup Enemy Number One: Fear

We all have fear: fear of the unknown; fear of rejection; fear of talking to people; fear of losing money; fear of making mistakes; fear of failure; fear of growing too much, too fast, and getting in over your head; and so on.

A lot of aspiring inventor-entrepreneurs let their fear get the better of them, allowing it to hold them back or even paralyze them. I can understand that. I've had a lot of fear over the years. I still have it! But I think fear can be either an enemy or an ally of success. Your body's natural response to fear is fight or flight, so it can compel you to either run from or fight for what you want.

Let me tell you a little bit about my fears.

All through grade school, high school, and college, I struggled with a learning disability that made academics difficult for me. It also made me feel insecure. Insecurity is a type of fear that can either discourage you from even trying or motivate you to prove yourself. For me, I think it was a little of both. When I took an art class in college, I found a passion for working with my hands and realized I would struggle doing anything else. So I became an art major, and that was a game-changer!

When I left college, without a degree, I was afraid no one would hire me because I thought I had no marketable skills. So I started making things and selling them at street fairs. I loved every minute of it. But I lived with constant fear, because if I made something and it didn't sell, I couldn't eat or pay my bills.

Then, when I was 27, I got my first real job at a startup toy company, Worlds of Wonder. I was scared out of my wits at first. But I learned a lot at WOW and met my wife there. Janice is the most brilliant woman I've ever met. She went to Stanford and has an MBA from Northwestern. She's everything I wish I could be.

After leaving WOW, we moved to Modesto, a small town in northern California, and raised our family. In the beginning, I worked mostly at home and sometimes at Kinko's, coming up with simple ideas and licensing them to manufacturers. Meanwhile, Janice held executive-level positions at Clorox before being hired as vice president of marketing at E&J Gallo Winery, becoming the highest-ranking woman in marketing in the company's history. I would go to these company parties, where everyone had MBAs from the best schools in the country. There I was, a dropout from San Jose State University, who for years made stuffed animals and sold them at street fairs and now designed and licensed toys and novelty items. My wife had this big job and big salary; we had this big house and all this fancy stuff. How could I live up to that? I had a lot of self-doubt. So I was always just very quiet . . . until I coached a kids' basketball team.

At the end of the season, Janice said, "Steve, you need to tell parents how their kids did." I thought, *How can I get up and talk to a group of parents?* Do you know the kind of paralyzing fear that makes your hands sweat and your knees shake? That's how I felt. But I got up there and talked, and I found my voice a little bit.

Later, after I'd successfully licensed several of my ideas, I started speaking to inventors' groups about my passion for coming up with simple ideas and bringing them to market. That's when I really found my voice—and another passion: teaching other people how to bring their simple ideas to market, too. I realized I have a purpose, a reason to be here and to play the biggest game in the world!

So I know what fear is, but over the years I've developed methods to fight it. And I'm going to share them with you in this book, so that you, too, can play the biggest game in the world and come out on top.

Why I Took the Leap and Started a Business with One Simple Idea

When I cofounded Hot Picks, I was 50 years old and had been successfully licensing my ideas to companies for about 20 years. People often ask me why I went from letting licensees do all the work and assume all the risks while I sat back and collected royalties to taking on all the risks and responsibilities myself. And why did I do that at age 50?

Fear had a lot to do with it. My biggest product, Spinformation, had stopped bringing in royalties, and I needed to replace that income. It was more than that, though. I'd had a good run with the labels, but I was bored with the product and losing interest. For a number of years, the royalties were extremely good; I could come and go as I pleased, and I had people working for me. But parts of it weren't perfect. I had lost a lot of control over the product and its trajectory, and the label was too expensive to manufacture. By the time the royalties disappeared, I wanted to do something different, but that old fear crept back in. I kept wondering, *What am I going to do now?* To add to my fear, my wife had left her job at Gallo to raise our three kids, so there was no financial cushion.

At about that time, Rob Stephani reappeared in my life. Like me, Rob had that entrepreneur spirit. Unlike me, he was a great businessperson and knew how to run a business from top to bottom. It was fun getting reacquainted as adults, and we would get together to talk and share information.

One day, we were talking about this guy in town who was selling a lot of guitar picks, Dave Khinoo, known as EBE Dave. We couldn't believe someone could be making so much money with a guitar pick. It was just a casual conversation between friends, but in the weeks that followed, I kept thinking about guitar picks. Even though I'm not a musician and knew nothing about guitars, my creative juices were turned on and flowing in the direction of guitar picks! One thing led to another, and I came up with the idea to slightly change the shape of a guitar pick. I still wasn't thinking about starting a business. But that's exactly what happened.

Initially, I thought we'd license the idea. But the more Rob and I talked about and looked into it, the more we thought, *Maybe we can bring this to market ourselves. Maybe we should start our own business.* Rob could handle the manufacturing, distribution, and administrative side of the business, and I could handle the design, marketing, and selling.

That got me to thinking about my first experiences as an entrepreneur, selling Softies at street fairs and in my retail store. I didn't make a lot of money, but it was one of the best times of my life. I was in charge, and it felt great when someone bought my product. Although it had all the basic elements of a small business, I lacked the confidence and know-how to take it to the next level: getting my products manufactured and into mass market stores all over the country.

When I came up with the idea for Hot Picks, I was older, wiser, and a bit more confident. I had a simple idea I was passionate about, the desire to be in charge, the thirst to learn what I didn't know, and the gumption to take the leap. So I did, and we rocked it!

Keep It Simple

O NE OF the main reasons product-based startups fail is because the idea is too big: it's too new and complicated for the market to grasp and buy; it's too difficult and expensive to produce. It doesn't matter how clever an idea is if no one wants to buy the product, no one can produce it, and you can't make any money on it. That's why I encourage people to start small and with a simple idea.

What Is a Simple Idea?

A simple idea is any new product that is easy to communicate, make, and sell. It makes sense to consumers, buyers, and vendors alike, and it fits easily into their lives, stores, and operations.

Many successful simple ideas are an improvement, enhancement, or incremental change to an existing product within a proven market. Making a small change to an existing product and for the same market niche is usually the smartest, simplest way to get into the game. But it's not the only way. You can put a unique twist on an existing product and target it for a different market niche. Take, for example, Celebri-Ducks, which transformed the quintessential little rubber ducky into a line of high-quality rubber ducks created in the images of various celebrities, which are marketed primarily as collectibles for adults rather than as toys for children.

It is also possible to bring a first-of-its-kind simple idea to market as long as it solves a common problem in a unique way and is relatively easy and affordable to produce. Chances are, you'll have to jump through additional hoops, work harder, and spend more than others to get it made and onto store shelves. But if the product has strong market and profit potential and you can swing it, the effort can be worth it. That was the case with Buzzy—the first medical device of its kind that takes the sting out of injections and intravenous jabs by applying gentle vibration and a cold compress to the area. As a mother, pain researcher, and pediatric emergency doctor, inventor/founder Amy Baxter knew the market and the technology for relieving minor pain. Even though Amy's idea was innovative, it was simple to make and sell, and she had the knowledge, passion, and credibility to make it happen.

Whether your product is revolutionary or evolutionary, your risks are lower and your chances of success are higher if it's a simple idea. Even better if it hits all the marks of a winning simple idea:

It is a consumable, collectible, or commonly used item. A great simple idea is something people will buy more than once. The best is if it's also something they'll buy for others. Repeat sales are a very good thing.

It has a large market. The product needs to solve a common problem or have universal appeal to a big, ready-made market so that it can be sold without having to educate the market or create a new market. It's something you would expect to find on the shelves of the largest retailers catering to that audience and carrying that product category.

It has a unique benefit you can show easily and customers can get instantly. Shelf space for "me-too" (very similar to other products) and "brand-new" products is extremely limited. Some wholesalers and retailers want nothing to do with them, and many consumers instinctively go for a sure thing they are familiar with. So, to get their attention and interest, a new or reimagined product has to offer something consumers want that competitive products don't offer.

It has a "wow" factor! A simple idea that is innovative, exciting, fun, fascinating, beautiful, or extraordinary in some way has a higher potential for success than one that fills a market need but is ho-hum. Novelty trumps ordinary every time.

It is small in size. Shelf space in retail is extremely valuable, so if your product has a small footprint, stores can more easily make room for it. An item that is relatively small and lightweight is also easier to ship and store than a big, heavy, awkwardly shaped item. We could store a million Hot Picks underneath a table. They were easy and inexpensive to ship, and super-easy to demonstrate. I could put a whole selection of Hot Picks in my pocket and show them to people wherever I went.

It can be made with existing technologies and common materials. When a product is easy and inexpensive to manufacture, it is easier and faster to bring to market. There is also less risk. You need to look into the feasibility, availability, and costs of both the manufacturing processes and the materials needed to make your product.

It has your stamp all over it. Most people assume you need to patent your idea. Given how long it takes patents to issue these days and the reality that it is possible to design around almost any patent, I'm not sure how important patents are. Perceived ownership is definitely important, but patents are debatable. There are other ways to protect your idea. I think it's more important to make sure your idea is unique and to get it out there quickly. Speed to market rules!

It has a good profit margin. The only simple idea worth pursuing is one that can be made at a cost and sold at a price that covers your costs and makes a decent profit. We were able to make Hot Picks for a few cents apiece and sell them for about $1 apiece (about $0.75 higher than our competitors' picks). That's a high profit margin. The idea was definitely worth bringing to market. It's not worth it if you have to undercut your prices to play the game. If you have to compete on price, you've already lost the battle.

Creating a Product That Will Sell

Most people invent backwards. They create a product and then try to find a market for it, rather than identifying a market opportunity and creating a product to fill it. That is especially true of inventor-entrepreneurs, who tend to create products they personally want, need, or like, giving little or no thought to who will buy them, where they'll be purchased, and why someone would buy the product. Some go so far as to bring their ideas to market—prototyping, patenting, producing, and promoting them—without first indentifying and testing the market, or even confirming there is one for their products.

Creating a product you would buy is one thing; creating a product you can sell is another. When you're investing all your blood, sweat, and tears into bringing a product to market, you want assurance that stores will carry it and consumers will buy it. You can't rely on guesses and assumptions, nor on what your family, friends, and colleagues think. You need current, real-world information. You need market research.

With a simple idea, you don't need to hire a hotshot (and expensive) marketing consultant, buy professionally compiled (and expensive) market data, or conduct fancy (and expensive) market research, analyses, and testing. There are faster, simpler ways to study and test the market that you can do yourself—and most are free!

Study the Marketplace

Before you get into the game, you have to understand it and have a strategy to win it. You need to know who your potential customers are, what they are buying, where they are buying it, and why they are buying it. You also need to know what's going on in your industry: where the opportunities for innovation and growth are, what the barriers to entry are, who the major players are, and which companies and products you'll be competing with.

You can learn everything you need to know about your industry, your market, and your competition by studying the marketplace. Here are some ways to study the market:

- Go shopping, anywhere and everywhere your potential customers might shop and your product might be sold, including big-box retailers, specialty stores, online stores, and mail-order catalogs.
- Ask a pro, anyone with expertise in whatever you need to know, including store managers, other inventor-entrepreneurs, manufacturers, industry gurus, and your own mentor.
- Read consumer reports and product reviews, online and in print.
- Browse websites, blogs, and publications that focus on market trends, such as Trendsetter.com and MindBranch.com.
- Browse websites of government agencies and market-research companies that study and report on consumer spending, population demographics, and your market niche.
- Browse online portals, forums, social media networks, and blogs that focus on your industry and product category.
- Read trade magazines, journals, and newsletters.
- Peruse consumer magazines that cater to your customer base, industry, and product category.
- Watch TV shopping shows. This is a good way to spot market trends and the most popular products.
- Network with trade associations, organizations, and clubs: visit their websites, go to their events, and talk to and ask questions of their representatives.
- Attend trade shows. This is probably the fastest way to get your finger on the pulse of the market, right up there with visiting retailers and searching the Internet. All you need to get into a trade show is your business card. If you sign up early online, you can sometimes get in free. You might also be able to get a pass from a local retailer or tag along with them, for free.

Get Up to Speed on Your Industry

Learn as much as you can about your industry and product category. Even if you have experience or knowledge in the area, you'll still need additional, current information to understand what's going on and where things are going. Things change fast in today's global market.

To get a handle on the industry and determine how your idea fits into it, you'll need to answer the following questions:

- What are the hot and emerging market trends in your industry and product category?
- Is the industry in a period of growth, decline, or stability?
- Are sales in your product category increasing, decreasing, or holding steady?
- Who are the major players in your product category?
- How many players are in your product category?
- Where and how is your product category sold?
- What is the range of products within your category?
- Are there products comparable to yours?

TIP

HOW TO DETERMINE YOUR INDUSTRY AND PRODUCT CATEGORY

If you're unsure which industry your product fits into, you can find out using one of the searchable databases of industry classifications and product categories on the Internet, such as the North American Industry Classification System (NAICS) index (see Chapter 6). I like the Google product category taxonomy; it's free, easy to use, and searchable online or downloadable as an Excel or text file.

Here is where Hot Picks fits into Google's product category taxonomy:

Arts & Entertainment > Hobbies & Creative Crafts > Musical Instruments & Accessories > String Instruments & Accessories > Guitar Accessories

When studying the market, many people look only at their product category (in this case, guitar accessories) and product type (e.g., guitar picks). But you can learn a lot about your customers and spot market opportunities you didn't even realize existed by extending your research to related product categories.

Stake Out Your Market

In order to innovate for the market, you have to target your market. You need to know who your potential consumers and retailers will be, why they'll want your product, and how much they'll be willing to pay for it. You will also need to determine the potential size of your market—how many stores and consumers might want your product.

One of the ways in which inventor-entrepreneurs sell themselves short is by not being diverse in their approach to identifying potential markets. They focus on just one group of consumers and one or two types of stores catering to that consumer group.

Then, there are smart go-getters such as Nancy Tedeschi. Like many of us, when Nancy came up with the idea for the SnapIt screw, she had in mind one application (hinge screws on eyeglasses) and one market (optical businesses). But she didn't stop there. She had the curiosity, open mind, and good sense to search for other markets—and she struck gold! She discovered a second application for the optical industry (lens screws on eyeglasses). Then, she found a new market, replacement eyeglass screws for consumers, which she sells at a variety of retailers, from drugstores to grocery stores, big-box retailers, discount stores, convenience stores, and airport shops. Now, she's mining new markets for a range of screws and fasteners for assemblies and machines in various industries.

So it pays to do some digging and identify every possible use, type of customer, and type of retailer for your product. Learn everything you can about each consumer group you're going after. Find out their demographics, lifestyles, and spending habits. Keep in mind that some products have both commercial (businesses) and consumer (public) applications.

Next, identify where your potential customers might buy your product. This is where many people get shortsighted. The marketplace is much bigger than your local mall and Amazon.com. Think local, regional, national, and international. Unearth every potential brick-and-mortar retailer that might sell your product. Find every potential merchant on the World Wide Web. Consider every conceivable sales channel for your product, such as television shopping channels, mail order catalogs, distributors, wholesalers, and exporters.

Could another brand use your product as a promotional item? Can you figure out a way to piggyback your idea off an item being widely used in a particular market? Take the fast-food industry as an example. Perhaps you invented a small toy that could be included in a kids' meal or a novelty cup that could be purchased along with a beverage. Fast-food restaurants such as McDonald's and Burger King are all over the world, and they sell billions of kids' meals and soft drinks a year. Even if you made only pennies per item, the sheer volume of potential sales would add up extremely quickly and could be very profitable.

When I was studying the market for Hot Picks, I used Google to research which types of stores sold guitar picks and how many stores of each type there were. I found tens of thousands of stores where Hot Picks could potentially be sold, including chain stores (like Hot Topic), big-box retailers (like Walmart), and convenience stores (like 7-Eleven). Our picks were also used as premiums for events such as the X Games and Jones Soda events.

Think outside the box, and find every viable market for your product.

Size Up the Competition

Often, it's what you don't know about other products in the market that knocks you out of the competition. If there are too many products comparable to yours, the market may be too saturated to allow room for your idea. If there are no products similar to yours, the market may not want or be ready for it. If your idea is a doppelganger of a product that already exists, the market may not welcome a me-too product.

On the other hand, what the competitors don't know about the market might give you an edge. If they are missing a hot market opportunity, you may be able to fill it with your product. Or maybe you can make a simple design change that gives your product a wow factor that makes your competitors' products pale in comparison!

To find a simple way to outshine the competition, you need to know what you're up against. That means studying the market to do the following:

- Make sure your idea or something very much like it isn't already out there.
- Identify existing products that might compete with yours.
- Identify the major players (brands).
- Determine the range of features and benefits among comparable products.
- Determine the price range for comparable products.
- Determine how comparable products are packaged.
- Determine where comparable products are sold.

When checking out the competition, note the different features, functions, and applications of comparable products. Pay extra-close attention to the benefits each competitive product offers consumers. Check out variations in design, quality, size, packaging, and price. Go shopping, and note where and how competitive products are displayed; ask store managers which products consumers are buying and which ones are languishing on the shelf.

Here are a few easy ways to check out the competition:

Go shopping. Browse local stores, online stores, catalogs, and Internet shopping portals.

Search Google Images, Google Product Search, and other reputable search engines. Click on the links to websites where you might find more detailed information. One of the advantages of using Google Images and Product Search is that they find all items on the Internet having those keywords/parameters on the Internet, not just sponsored links.

Go straight to the source: your competitors. Visit competing brands' websites, and check out their product pages, media pages, store locators, and wholesaler pages (and price lists, if they are posted). Read their product literature, visit their exhibits at trade shows, and tap into their social media networks.

Ask the experts. Check out trade magazines, industry newsletters, trade association websites, trade shows, blogs, and other places that follow and report on companies and products in your markets.

Find Your Competitive Edge

Once you've gathered all that information about your market niche, look at it closely to determine what the competition is doing right and what you could do better. Look for what's missing in the market and how you might fill the gap. Look for ways to stand out from the competition and win over customers.

When you're analyzing a comparable product, the most important thing to understand is the benefit it offers. What do consumers like about it? Why do they buy it? Is it the quality of the product? Certain bells and whistles? Brand awareness? Convenience? Customer service? Price?

When comparing your product with a competitive product, identify the unique benefit your product offers. How might you add more benefit? What benefits have your competitors missed? What consumers have they missed? The heavy hitters miss a lot. You just need to find a small opportunity, an incremental change to an existing product. Identify weaknesses you can solve, enhancements you can make, or new opportunities you can seize.

When we were studying the market for Hot Picks, we visited a lot of independent music stores and some chains. We noticed five or six major brands of guitar picks. We asked the store clerks which brand was the most popular; they all said the same thing: Dunlop, "the player's pick." Dunlop had endorsements from all the famous guitarists, and it had the biggest ads in the music magazines. Having been in the business for at least 40 years, it had great distribution and more products in stores than anyone else. It had done a wonderful job. But we noticed two things: the picks had little personality, and the packaging was bare bones. A few picks had a simple graphic or image of a band on them, but not many. Often, we found picks just piled up in tackle boxes that customers had to dig through. That's where we saw our in: we could go after the lack of style in guitar picks and make designs that really resonated with people, and we could package them in a distinctive way.

One beneficial thing that many big brands and design firms do is to watch people use the type of product they are interested in designing. You can do the same thing: observe people using a comparable product, and ask questions. What do they like? What do they dislike?

What would they like to see? It's a great way to spot opportunities for improvements and enhancements.

Look at the marketplace, too. Are there boring or outdated styles and materials you could update or replace? Could you use existing technology or materials in a new way? Is there an emerging trend or an underserved niche you could focus on?

Take heed of what you learn, and use it to innovate for the market. Keep working your design to iron out any weaknesses, to pump up the wow factor, and to find your competitive advantage—a clear and exciting benefit that grabs the consumers' attention and makes them want to open their wallets.

Do You Know . . . Or Do You THINK You Know?

When I came up with the simple idea to form the contour of a guitar pick into novelty shapes, I knew in my bones we were on to something! Our strongest competitor was raking in a half million dollars a year making and selling guitar picks with the face of an alien printed on them, so we knew there was a market for novelty guitar picks. We knew people constantly replace their guitar picks and buy multiple picks at a time, therefore, we knew it was a sizable market. My partner, Rob Stephani, is a guitarist and owned a music store, so we also thought we knew our customers.

My first designs were shaped like women's bosoms and bottoms clad in bikinis and lingerie. Hot chicks and guitar picks—hence, Hot Picks! Sex, drugs, and rock 'n' roll, right? I thought guys would love them!

But two things went wrong: We couldn't get the flesh tones right, so the guitar picks didn't really look like bodies. And we didn't *really* know our customers.

You see, most of the people shopping for guitar picks weren't guys. They were moms and teenagers, and they weren't interested in hot-chick guitar picks. The stores where they shopped didn't want to carry them, either. So do you really know, or do you just *think* you know? Here's the rub: we would have known had I not skipped the first step in bringing a simple idea to market, the one I'd been practicing and preaching for years—study the market!

Fortunately, we'd spent only a couple hundred dollars on the girlie designs we couldn't sell. But then we didn't know what else to put on the guitar picks. This time I wasn't leaving it to chance, though. So I went to the mall to try to understand what kids thought was cool and wanted to buy.

One of the stores I visited was Hot Topic—a retail chain specializing in music- and pop culture-themed clothing and accessories for youth. Everywhere I looked, I saw skulls. When I spotted a sticker of a skull with a pointy chin, I instantly envisioned it as a guitar pick. I bought the sticker and showed it to Rob. Could he play guitar with a pick shaped like that? He could, but being the true musician he is, he was hesitant to change the shape of the pick. He eventually came around.

But first we decided to do something smart: we came up with about a dozen designs and tested them on the market. We wanted young folks in music stores—rather than us, two 50-year-old guys—to decide their favorite designs before we created the molds and brought the product to market.

To determine which images might appeal to young people, I combed through music and entertainment magazines as well as magazines with a similar audience, such as skateboarders. I also checked out stores catering to that same demographic. I found several popular images that could be molded into the rounded-triangle shape of a guitar pick: devils, monster faces, human faces, animal faces, and of course, skulls. We drew up some designs and put together a product sheet.

We took the flyers and questionnaires to four local music stores. Every store clerk or manager who filled out the whole questionnaire would get $50, and each young person who mentioned his or her favorites would get a gift. The person behind the counter just had to write down each participant's name and address, and we would send that person the picks after we'd made them. It wasn't much, but it was an incentive. We got back all the questionnaires a week later.

It was clear which designs were most popular. Two were strong frontrunners: a skull and a zombie face. We started with the skull. Knowing one design is not enough on which to build a company, we soon added the zombie face that our focus group liked so well. Both were big sellers! We used those same two molds to create hundreds of designs—several different skulls and human faces, demons, vampires, Frankenstein's monster (and other monsters), a bulldog and other animal heads, crazy clowns, hearts, even Mickey Mouse. By the way, that first skull design continues to be a popular seller today.

You could say we picked a couple of winners. But actually our customers did!

Test the Market

Before you start spending your hard-earned money trying to bring your idea to market, you should test the waters to see whether consumers really want it. Although studying the market will give you a good idea of whether your product will sell, only potential customers can tell you whether it's a potential winner.

Find out what they think of your product. What do they like best and least about it? Have they owned or used a similar product? If so, how does your product compare? What do they like better about your product than a comparable product? What do they not like as well? Would they buy your product? How much would they be willing to pay for it?

Before you start showing your idea to the world, make sure you have some type of intellectual property protection, such as a trademark, copyright, and/or provisional patent application.

Here are several ways to test the market:

Ask consumers. Do a focus group or survey to ask people in your target audience what they think about your product. You can create a flyer that describes your product, shows a drawing or photo of it, and includes a few questions for people to answer.

They can then leave the flyers at the checkout counter of a local store, as we did with Hot Picks. Today, you could do a similar kind of survey on the Internet using social media, a blog, or an e-mail blast. Or you can simply walk around and ask people. You can pay companies to do focus groups, but doing that is very expensive, or you can conduct your own. Do some research on how to run an effective focus group or survey. You should always offer an incentive for people to do a good job. One time I bought pizza for a party and put my product on the table and videotaped the kids interacting with it.

Sell the product. Do a small production run of a hundred or so products and try to sell them at local retailers, online (e.g., your website, craigslist, eBay, Amazon.com), or possibly at a local street fair. Even if it costs you a couple of thousand dollars, that's not much compared to the money and time you would spend developing a product only to find out it's a flop. We did a small test run with Hot Picks (and quickly sold out!). Also, when I was selling my products at street fairs early in my career, I constantly made handmade prototypes to see which designs customers liked. I loved it, because I knew immediately if people wanted my product.

Ask someone who has done it before. Find one or more experienced entrepreneurs who have taken products to market in a related field (or even your field). Get to know them, and take them out for lunch or dinner or drinks. Tell them about your idea, show it to them.

Research the problem your product solves. Do a web search for the problem, need, or desire you think your idea will solve. How many people are talking about the problem, need, or desire? What are they saying? Is it really an issue? Check online discussion groups, boards, forums, and blogs; ask questions. You could even blog about the problem yourself and see what kind of responses you get.

Post an online ad. When you create an online ad using Google AdWords, Yahoo! Advertising Solutions, or AdCenter on

Bing, you specify key words that people might use to search your product type. Whenever a search is done using any of those key words, your ad will appear next to the search results. If your ad is clicked on (which is more likely to happen than if you were just listed in the search results), the person doing the search is directed to your website, where they can learn more about your product, request additional information, or perhaps fill out a short survey. You could even put a "Coming Soon!" banner and an order form on the page. Make sure to provide your e-mail address and/or phone number so people can contact you to indicate their interest. If you ask people to fill out a survey, offer a small reward for their effort.

Ask an angel investor. Find someone who is looking for ideas to invest in. You can find angel investors at speaking events for startups or online (for example, through LinkedIn.com). Ask these people if they would invest in your product or know anyone else who might. They are brutally honest, and they'll tell you what they think. It will be great feedback.

Run it by a potential licensee. Consider trying to license your idea to a company first. Of course, you will need to get a little intellectual property protection and have company representatives sign a nondisclosure agreement. Choose a company that sells products in your same category—complementary and related products, not products your product would compete with. Would that organization like to put your product in the company's product line? Licensees are in the trenches day in and day out, and they are going to be honest with you. If they say they would license it, that's a great sign you're onto something. It's also another option to consider.

I don't care how you test the market, just do it! You're going to feel a lot more comfortable pulling the trigger if you get a thumbs-up from people who would actually buy your product. You're also going to reduce your risks and increase your chances of success by testing the market and listening to what it tells you, modifying your idea to fit the market.

THE BEST TEST MARKET MONEY DIDN'T BUY

The only *real* way to test the market is to do a small production run, put the product out there, and see if it sells. If it does, you know you've got a winner. But most small startups are hesitant to spend the money or don't have the money to spend on a preproduction test run. Some don't know how to get a test run into the market where consumers can buy it. For some, it's completely off their radar. But bringing a product to market not knowing for certain whether it will sell is a big risk. So it's worthwhile to at least try to do an inexpensive test run and line up a prospective customer (or two) for it ahead of time. That's exactly what I did for a recent project, Spin Cups. To explain a little bit about this project, fast-food restaurants and convenience stores use thermoform cups for their fountain beverages. Spin Cups are thermoform cups with my rotating label, which can be used for promotions, games, and entertainment.

The goal: do a market test with no out-of-pocket costs and secure a contract with a prospective customer.

Here's what happened:

1. We built a prototype. We took a regular fast-food cold-beverage cup, printed the artwork on our own printer, and glued the label to the cup. It cost less than $100. It looked beautiful!

2. We showed the prototype to the prospective client. The client loved it. But there were questions asked we couldn't answer yet: How will the cup be manufactured? How much will it cost? The prospective client loved the product and wanted to carry it. But the client wanted to see the actual item. I was not surprised.

3. The client didn't give us a purchase order on a prototype; clients never do.

4. We found a cup supplier that would change the cup mold at no cost to us, a $3,000 value. He would also preprint the cup base at no cost to us, a $2,000 value.

5. We found a label supplier that would print test labels at no cost to us, a value of $2,000 to $3,000.

6. We found a label machinery supplier that would do the test run on its machinery at no cost to us, a value of $2,000 to $3,000.

The preproduction samples were done. They were beautiful. Now, we could return to the prospective client, show the finished product to the buyer, and get the order. We resolved our production issues and had pricing for the cups.

We got all three suppliers to pay for their own R&D (research and development) for our project because they knew we had a qualified buyer who was very interested in our cup after seeing our prototype. We didn't go to the biggest suppliers; we went to the suppliers who were ranked number three or four. Suppliers a little further down the totem pole are hungry for the business, and were willing to do our $10,000+ preproduction run for free. That was the best money I never spent.

Creating a Product That Is Simple to Produce

It doesn't matter how many people want to buy your idea if the product can't be manufactured or is too difficult or expensive to make. This information is crucial to know before you design it, prototype it, patent it, and market it.

You don't need to become a manufacturing expert, and you don't yet need to get exact price quotes. You just need a basic understanding of the materials, processes, and associated costs involved in manufacturing and packaging your product. One of the big advantages of a simple idea is that the technology needed to manufacture it already exists, which you've confirmed by studying the market.

You can do some preliminary legwork to find out whether and how your idea might be manufactured by talking to someone who has brought a similar product to market or is very knowledgeable of your industry, such as an expert you find at a trade show or trade association. Other resources for finding out how something is manufactured are websites such as Howstuffworks.com (http://www.howstuffworks.com) and the free online encyclopedia HSIM (How Stuff Is Made; http://www.howstuffismade.org).

Ultimately, you want to talk with at least one, preferably two or three, potential contract manufacturers. You can find contract manufacturers through trade associations, online directories and portals, and online searches. You'll need to describe your idea and show the manufacturer a drawing and possibly a mock-up or prototype of your product. Before you do that, make sure you've filed a provisional patent application (PPA), have typed "Patent Pending" on your drawings and spec sheets, and had the contractor sign a nondisclosure agreement (NDA). (For more on provisional patent applications and nondisclosure agreements, see Chapter 4.)

Find out whether the contract manufacturer can produce your product in its facility. If this can be done, get a price quote for different volumes of production—for example, 1,000 units, 10,000 units, 100,000 units, or higher, wherever the cost breaks are. Find out whether there will be additional setup costs; some manufacturers absorb capital expenditures for retooling and new equipment. The manufacturer should also be able to tell you what local, state, and national regulations you'll need to comply with and the costs associated with them.

If the contract manufacturer can't produce your idea, ask why. With that information, you may be able to redesign or reengineer your idea to make it doable for the manufacturer. For example, I reworked my spin label to reduce the manufacturing cost by more than 50 percent. You can also ask the contract manufacturer if there are any other companies that might be able to produce your idea.

Sometimes, this research will blow an idea right out of the water. The beauty of a simple idea is that, more often than not, it is possible and profitable to get it made.

Is It a Money-Maker?

Every link in the chain needs to make money on your product: your manufacturer, distributor, retailers, and you. So it's important to know whether your idea is a potential money-maker *before* you try to bring it to market. To do that, you'll need to estimate your production costs (manufacturing and packaging), your wholesale prices (what distributors and retailers will pay you), and your retail list price. You also need to estimate the number of units you could sell in a year. Then, you'll need to do some math to determine whether your idea is a potential money-maker . . . or money pit.

A simple way to estimate your manufacturer's suggested retail price (MSRP), or retail list price, is to multiply your per-unit production cost by 5 (the 1-to-5 rule). For example, if your manufacturing and packaging cost is $2 per unit, your retail price should be $10. Another way to set the retail price is to simply double the wholesale price, a pricing method known as *keystoning*. Keystoning usually works when you are selling straight to the retailer. Of course, customers have to be willing to pay the retail price you come up with, which you should have determined by studying the market.

Superstores (e.g., Walmart) and warehouse clubs (e.g., Costco) usually want a lower wholesale price or an extra discount.

If you use a distributor, you'll need to build a commission into the price. A pricing formula commonly used for distributors is the 50/25/10 discount: 50 percent of the retail price, less 25 percent of that amount, less 10 percent of that amount. For example, here is the 50/25/10 calculation for a product retailing for $10: 50 percent of $10 = $5, less 25 percent of $5 ($1.25) = $3.75, less 10 percent of $3.75 ($0.38) = $3.37. The distributor's price would be $3.37. If you're using one or more distributors, you may want to set your retail list price a little higher than the keystone (50 percent) rate.

Now, it's time to do the math:

1. Determine your per-unit production cost (manufacturing + packaging costs).
2. Determine your average per-unit *wholesale price*. (For example, distributor wholesale price + mass retailer wholesale price + retail wholesale price, divided by three.)
3. Determine your average per-unit *gross profit*. (Subtract your per-unit production cost from your average per-unit wholesale price.)

4. Estimate your *weekly sales* (number of units sold) per week in each store.
5. Determine your estimated weekly sales, in units. (Multiply the number of stores in your market by the number of units you expect to sell each week.)
6. Determine your estimated *annual sales*, in units. (Multiply your estimated weekly sales by 52 weeks.)
7. Determine your estimated *annual gross profit*. (Multiply your estimated annual sales by the average wholesale price.)
8. Determine your *gross profit margin*. (Divide your gross profit by your wholesale price.)

WIDGET: COST BREAKDOWN

This worksheet shows the estimated production costs, pricing, sales, and profits for an example widget product in a box. This example is for illustration purposes only.

Retail list price: $4.99
Manufacturing and packaging costs (per box):

Widget	$0.18
Box	$0.16
Instructions	$0.01
Labor	$0.20
Shipping package	$0.03
Total cost	$0.58

	Distributors	Mass Retailers	Retailers	Average
Production cost	$0.58	$0.58	$0.58	$0.58
Wholesale price	$1.69	$1.90	$2.15	$1.91
Gross profit	$1.11	$1.32	$1.57	$1.33
Gross margin	66%	69%	73%	69%

Sales/profit projections:

10,000 stores × 1 sale per week × 52 weeks =
520,000 units sold for the year

520,000 sales × $1.91 (average sale price) =
$993,200 gross profit for the year

Remember, all of your other business expenses—insurance, licenses, marketing, taxes, patents, office, warehouse, payroll, supplies, and so on—will come out of your gross profit. At this point, you don't need to identify all the costs of doing business. You just need to get a feel for whether your estimated gross profit will be enough to cover your bills and put money in your pocket.

If the numbers aren't there, it doesn't necessarily mean your idea isn't a potential money-maker. You may be able to reduce your production costs by tweaking or redesigning your product and/or the packaging. Just make sure those changes don't undermine the marketability of your idea or undercut the price consumers will pay for it. At the end of the day, you need assurance that your idea will sell at a price and in sufficient quantities, and can be made at a cost that gives you the profit you want.

• • •

The easiest, fastest, safest, and surest way to build a profitable business is to start small and with a simple idea: simple to sell; simple to make; and simple to ship, store, and shelve. If you keep it simple and do the market research and testing to make sure your idea is marketable, doable, and profitable, you can play the biggest game in the world and come out a winner.

Watch Your Back

$\mathbf{A}$ s a first-time inventor-entrepreneur, you might be feeling a little intimidated about competing with established brands and big companies. The worries of being a rookie in this high-stakes game are probably preying on your mind: Will retailers let you into the game? Will competitors play fairly? Will someone beat you to the punch with a similar idea? Will vendors give you a good deal and good service? Will customers notice your product and give it a chance? Will someone steal your idea?

The fear of someone stealing their idea is the main reason so many people run out and file a patent as soon as they lock in on their idea. They think the only or best way to protect an idea is to patent it before showing it to anyone. But that would mean withholding your idea from the very people whose help you need to bring your idea to market: your mentor, the industrial designer who does your drawing or prototype, your contract manufacturer, the graphic designer who creates your packaging, the consumers in your test market, and the retailers who will carry your product.

Keep in mind that the cost typically ranges from $10,000 to $20,000 and takes from three to four years for a patent to issue. Consider, too, that the idea you start out with is always different than the product you end up with. Most products, even simple ideas, go through several design changes between concept and finished product. When you file a patent early on, you often have to file several patents before the process is over.

Meanwhile, as you're going through all that time, trouble, and money trying to patent your idea to keep someone from stealing it, someone else may come out with a comparable product and grab your place in the market before you even get there. Or the needs and tastes of your target audience will change, and the market for your idea will evaporate before your product materializes. Remember: the first to market wins!

You definitely need to safeguard your idea—your *intellectual property* (IP). But there are faster, easier, and cheaper ways to do that than by getting a patent. Yes, some ideas still need to be patented. But you have more control over whether and when to file a patent than you might think. You certainly don't have to wait until your patent issues to start making and selling your product. In fact, for most simple ideas, you *shouldn't* wait.

Before examining the basics on patents and other forms of IP protection, let's look at a few other ways to protect your idea and your business.

Outsmart the Competition

How do you compete with large companies and established brands? I don't know that you really need to compete with them. In fact, I think it's foolish to try to beat them at their own game with a product too similar to theirs. One of the most effective ways to protect an idea is to come out with a product that nobody else had the ingenuity or ability to create. The *only* way to claim and defend IP rights to an idea is to design something that is unique.

You see, the heavy hitters prioritize going after the big dollars. That's their business model, but it doesn't have to be yours. At large companies, the process for bringing a new product to market is so long, complicated, and expensive that they often don't bother with simple ideas that an entrepreneur or small company might be able to bring to market quickly and profitably.

Being small is not the disadvantage many people think it is. Being small is great! You can act fast and make decisions unilaterally. You can grab golden opportunities large companies miss or dismiss. And the big leaguers leave a lot of opportunities on the table.

So, instead of trying to go toe-to-toe with competitors, look for opportunities to do something fresh and different, and then bring your innovative idea to market before someone else does. You can find that competitive edge by studying the market. The following are a few other simple strategies you can use to outsmart the competition.

Exploit Your Strengths and Your Competitors' Weaknesses

Find your competitors' weaknesses, and then take advantage of them by finding your strengths. This is the fun part. Study the products, merchants, and customers of your top competitors. What key benefit(s) do they provide? What features, functions, and/or audience have they missed or perhaps intentionally not gone after? What could you do better? What unique value or wow factor could you provide? What underserved market segment could you target? If you look carefully, you'll see opportunities to outshine the competition and fill a void in the market.

First to Market Trumps First to Patent
Annette Giacomazzi/CastCoverZ

I'm often asked if I've patented my product. The answer is no. I decided it would be too expensive to patent it and too expensive to defend the patent if somebody copied the product. Pursuing a patent would have generated a lot of negative energy and taken a lot of time. I wanted to get my product to market as quickly as possible. To further distinguish my brand, I came out of the gate providing extraordinary customer service. Although many people followed me, I was the first to market, and CastCoverZ is still the leader in cast covers.

Be Creative

Use your creativity to design a product that has a unique benefit and a wow factor your target audience can't resist and your competition can't easily and quickly mimic. No matter how great your first idea is and how well it sells, one version of one product is rarely enough to sustain and grow a business. So you'll need to keep those creative juices flowing to continually improve and expand your brand—and to keep competitors off your back.

Whether designing a new product or updating an existing product, I look for simple ways to provide a unique benefit to the consumer. I look for styles, materials, and technologies that are not being used. I love looking at products, especially traditional ones, and asking, "How could this be more useful? How could it be more fun? How can I make someone's life easier or put a smile on someone's face?"

At Hot Picks, we continually created new designs using the latest trends in colors, patterns, and images as well as the most enduring characters (such as Disney characters). With our line of lenticular designs, we changed up the material. Lenticular printing produces a three-dimensional image that looks like it moves, or morphs, from one image to another. The technology has been around since the 1940s, but it had never been used on guitar picks! Because we innovated constantly and moved quickly, we were able to stay ahead of any competition, attract new customers, and increase repeat sales from existing customers. After a while, our products became collectible, not just utility items for guitar players.

Stay Current

One of the best ways to watch your back is to stay ahead of the pack— to look ahead, think ahead, and design ahead! That's why it's important to keep up with what's going on in the market, your industry, and the world. Browse popular magazines. Watch popular movies, TV shows, and online videos. Go shopping. Look for emerging trends and new technologies. Then use your creativity and agility to create products that wow and benefit your target audience.

If you keep your brand exciting and relevant, you'll get more customers, sell more products, make more money, and stay ahead of the competition.

KNOCKING OUT A KNOCKOFF
Leslie Haywood/Grill Charms

I was a little frustrated but also a little flattered when someone knocked me off. Fortunately, their product is inferior to mine and hit the market three years after mine. Theirs is made of aluminum, which I actually considered because it's so cheap. But after researching different materials, I didn't feel comfortable putting aluminum in food. So I went with food- and surgical-grade stainless steel. Grill Charms are not only safer, they're also more attractive and durable than the knockoffs. Because I was the first to market and had a higher-quality product, I left my copycats in the dust.

Cater to Your Customer

The number one way to one-up the competition is to make your customer your number one priority. To do that, you have to really know and understand your customers.

If you know your customers, you'll end up loving them. You'll want to please them by designing products they want and need. You'll give them the best prices you can, and provide them with the most amazing customer service possible. As a result, your customers will love you back. They'll buy your products over and over again and recommend your products. The more tuned in and responsive you are to your customers, the more loyal they will become. If another product comes out that is similar to yours, your loyal customers will still purchase yours. They will look to you for product enhancements and new products and watch your back.

Be Frugal and Resourceful

One of the smartest things you can do to defend your slice of the pie is to keep your costs low. I never want to compete with lower-priced products, and I always want to have the leeway to give incentives and free product. If you're frugal and resourceful, you can offer a great product at a competitive price and still have a good profit margin.

Being frugal and resourceful also helps you be agile, enabling you to get new and improved products out there quickly. Speed is your ally! If you can beat your competitors to market, that's about the best protection you can get.

So do whatever you can to keep a lid on spending and to do more with less. Bootstrap it, outsource, barter, get freebies, work smarter, pinch pennies, and so on.

RUBBER DUCKIE, YOU'RE NUMBER ONE!

Craig Wolfe/CelebriDucks

No matter how big or small you are, what industry you're in, or how long you've been around, you've got to watch your back. I address those concerns with speed and agility. That's one of the things CelebriDucks is known for: we can turn on a dime. We can hit deadlines no other company can make—like designing and producing 2,000 Conan O'Brien ducks to launch his new show.

I also knew no one else would spend money on licensing celebrity images or on packaging. My competitors all produce cheapies and fight over pennies. If you're innovative and fast enough, you can create your own niche. You become the standard. If anyone does try to knock you off, they usually fail because you've already locked up the market. We own the commercial art rubber duck market!

I also run lean and mean. I have no debt and very little overhead, and I'm a master at outsourcing. I could run this whole business with a cell phone and a laptop from a beach in Waikiki! Many new and aspiring inventor-entrepreneurs want to spend, spend, spend. The landscape is littered with companies with unbelievable sales volumes that went belly-up because they took on excessive debt and overhead. My motto is: it's not how much money you make; it's how much money you keep.

Build Partnerships

Another way to protect your idea and your business is to build solid relationships with everyone you work with: vendors, retailers, manufacturing reps, customers, and even competitors.

I suggest trying to form relationships with some of the major players in your industry. Maybe you can convert them from competitors to allies by throwing some business their way. If your idea doesn't directly compete with their products, you might be able to use them as a distributor or contract manufacturer. If they view you as an ally and not as a direct competitor, they can also help you understand the industry and connect you with other resources.

At Hot Picks, we took our leading competitors right out of the game by building other relationships with them. We contracted with Dunlop to make our guitar picks, and we used another manufacturer as a distributor, which kept both companies from ripping us off. Even though the two companies made guitar picks, our picks didn't compete directly with the manufacturer's and that company was earning income off us. This eliminated any reason for competition.

Although we had no IP protection on our lenticular line (apart from being an exclusive Disney licensee on some of the designs), we threw so much business at Extreme Graphics, the contract manufacturer for our lenticular picks, that I doubt they ever considered supplying anyone else with lenticular picks. I'm sure people there realized they would have lost our trust and our business.

One of the largest producers we partnered with was Fender. Because of our openness to talk with other people, Fender actually contacted us about buying lenticular guitar picks from us. Fender didn't want to get new tooling and start a relationship with Extreme Graphics, so they came to us. We got the product from Extreme Graphics and sold it to Fender for a little more than we paid for it. If we hadn't done it for Fender, the company would have done it anyway. So, even though their lenticular picks competed with ours, by working as Fender's supplier, we made money on the picks we supplied, which prevented us from being copied.

Whoever your vendors are, develop a one-on-one relationship and keep an open line of communication with each one. Make sure it's a win-win situation for both parties, and pay on time. One of the reasons I suggest trying to find contract manufacturers in the United States is because it's easier to develop and sustain a closer relationship with them.

You can also leverage the power of a big company by licensing a name or image to which they own the rights. Becoming a Disney licensee and being the official guitar pick of B.C. Rich Guitars legitimized us and gave us protection, preventing anyone else from producing and marketing a Mickey Mouse or skull pick.

It is very important to build strong relationships with your retailers— from the smallest to the biggest. Your retailers are on the front line, and they can provide great protection. Send them good product, give them good service and prices, and stay connected with them. Check in regularly to ask how they are doing and what they need. If your retailers feel like you have their back, they'll be more apt to have yours. If others come around with products that are similar to yours, retailers will be more likely to pass on them or to at least give your product more and better space than they will to the competition. If others approach the retailers with knockoffs, they'll turn them away and let you know about it.

Working directly and closely with our Hot Picks retailers helped protect us from me-too products. For example, we had talked with a manufacturer in China about making our skull picks, and when we decided not to go with that company, it made them anyway! It tried to sell skull picks on eBay, but we were policing that website and spotted the knockoff immediately. Because of our relationship with eBay, as soon as Hot Picks informed that auction site of the violation, it booted the manufacturer off the site.

When building relationships, make sure everyone is on the same page and has the same expectations. Be personable and professional. Pick up the phone. Don't rely solely on e-mail. Follow up, and keep your promises. Others will treat you well in return and help you get to the level you desire.

Last, but not least, develop strong relationships with your customers. This is an area big companies tend to neglect and many smaller companies don't fully develop. Building a good customer relationship starts with providing a good product at a good price. To create a loyal customer who comes back for more and sends other customers to you, you have to provide great customer service. When you give your customers a great product, a good price, and fantastic customer service, they will choose your product over a competitor's every time. They may even let you know when someone's infringing on your idea.

Protect Your Idea

The traditional line of thinking says you need a patent to protect your idea. I just don't think that's true anymore. It is possible to design around a patent, and there's no way to anticipate every small change or improvement that can be made to your idea. Relying on a patent to protect your idea is foolish. So is waiting for a patent to issue before you start making and selling your product. Although you may want or need to get a patent at some point, you would be wise to start off by getting the immediate protection you can afford and getting your product to market as quickly as possible.

Intellectual property protection is a broad and complicated field, and it varies from country to country. It also can be a costly and lengthy process, so you want to make sure you really need it and know which kind(s) you need and when. Patents, trademarks, and copyrights are used for different purposes. You might need a copyright for one aspect of your idea, a trademark for another aspect, and a patent for another. Or you might find you don't need any IP protection, although I usually recommend at least a provisional patent application, or PPA (see "The Power of Patent Pending," later in this chapter), for most simple ideas. It really depends on what idea you have, and you won't be able to make a decision until after you've educated yourself on IP protection and perhaps consulted with a patent attorney.

Before you contact a patent attorney or show your idea to anyone, I suggest you learn as much as you can about the types of IP available in your country. Good sources of information include the U.S. Patent and

Trademark Office (http://www.uspto.gov); David Pressman's books, *Patent It Yourself* and *Patent Pending in 24 Hours*; and IPWatchdog (http://www.ipwatchdog.com), the website and blog of patent attorney and professor Gene Quinn.

Meanwhile, I suggest you get and start using two tools every inventor-entrepreneur needs: *inventor's logbooks* and *nondisclosure agreements* (NDAs).

Inventor's Logbook

From the moment you come up with your idea, you should start documenting everything you think, learn, and do in a notebook. An accurate and detailed inventor's logbook is your first line of defense in protecting and defending your idea. Its purpose is to provide a chronological record that proves your idea is 100 percent yours.

Begin by documenting the date you came up with the idea and a detailed description of the idea. Record and date every consecutive step you take from that point on; include detailed notes on testing, prototypes, test production runs, drawings, computer-aided design (CAD) renderings, technical specifications, computations, and notes from conversations and meetings with manufacturers and patent attorneys. Retain receipts for materials, drawings, prototypes, professional services, samples, and so on, and keep them in or near the logbook.

To be legally viable, an inventor's logbook must adhere to the following standards:

- The journal must be bound so that any removed pages can be detected. Never use a spiral notebook. Instead, use a perfect-bound composition notebook so that pages cannot be easily removed.
- No lines or pages can be skipped.
- The full name of any participant in the process must be recorded along with the date and nature of their involvement (each incident).
- Each entry must be dated and handwritten in ink (not pencil). It cannot be typed.

- Each entry must be signed and dated by a third party, signifying that he or she understands the contents of that entry. This person can be anyone other than an immediate family member who can read and understand what you have written in the logbook.

When the ownership of an idea is in dispute, the person with the most detailed and accurate logbook, which verifies the date the idea was conceived and proves that the inventor worked continuously to design and develop it, is more likely to win. That inventor's odds are even better if he or she has also filed a PPA.

Nondisclosure and Work-for-Hire Agreements

In most countries, a mutual nondisclosure agreement signed by the inventor-entrepreneur and a person with whom the inventor shows or discusses his idea prevents the public disclosure of the idea before (and after) a PPA or nonprovisional patent application is filed. If you haven't filed for patent protection, I suggest using a nondisclosure agreement whenever you show your idea to anyone other than your immediate family and most trusted friends.

For any people performing tasks related to your product—for example, contract manufacturers, industrial designers, graphic artists, or CAD engineers—you definitely need them to sign an NDA. You may also want them to sign a *work-for-hire agreement* stating that any work they perform on your behalf belongs wholly and exclusively to you. That way, they have no claim to your invention/product.

Your attorney can draw up an NDA and work-for-hire agreement for you or advise you on what to include if you create them yourself or modify documents you have purchased (or downloaded free from the Internet).

This is crucial: show your idea only to people you can trust—and only if and when they need to see or hear about it in order to give you the information or assistance you need. Keep certain details of your design to yourself until you have a PPA and are ready to start making and selling your product. Then, reveal only what that person needs to know to help you move forward with your idea.

Exposing your idea to the wrong people can enable someone to design around it and beat you to market with a similar product. If the person signed your NDA and you filed either a PPA or nonprovisional patent application before showing that person your idea, you'll have evidence of intellectual property infringement. But who needs the headache and expense of proving an idea is yours? Few inventor-entrepreneurs have the resources and time to fight and recover from an IP infringement. If it happens, a better option might be to change the design and come up with something even better.

There is also risk in promoting your idea too soon. A product can be touted as being "new" for a relatively short period of time. So if you spread the word way before your product comes out, you could blow your only opportunity to publicize your idea. Meanwhile, you could also give your competitors the opportunity to beat you to market with a similar product.

Copyright

The U.S. copyright law protects IP rights to any published and unpublished "original works" of authorship and artwork that is "fixed in a tangible medium of expression," which means it has been documented or recorded or exists in some tangible form. Things that can be copyrighted include websites, jingles, TV commercials, print and Internet ads, audio and video recordings, and graphic, pictorial, photographic, and sculptural images. Things that *cannot* be copyrighted include ideas, processes, formulas, recipes, names, slogans/tag lines, facts, research, and unrecorded speeches/presentations. We copyrighted the graphic designs on our Hot Picks, which enabled us to stay ahead of the copycat crowd.

A copyright registered with the United States Copyright Office grants ownership rights of the original work to the individual who created it or the company that commissioned it. The copyright owner has the exclusive right to do, or authorize others to do, the following things for a specified period of time:

- Reproduce the work
- Distribute the work

- Create derivative works
- Publicly perform the work or recordings of the work via digital transmission
- Publicly display the work

Copyright protection for an individual (such as an artist) remains in force from the date of first publication or registration, whichever comes first, until 70 years after the creator's death. If the work is created by or for a company, copyright protection extends for 120 years from the date of creation or 95 years from the date of the first publication, whichever is shorter.

It is no longer necessary to register a copyright or affix the copyright mark (the symbol © followed by the owner's name and date of creation/publication) on the copyrighted item. However, I think it's a good idea to do so, because it makes it easier and faster to prove ownership, and filing a copyright is simple and affordable. You can submit the application on the U.S. Copyright Office website (http://www.copyright.gov/). An electronically filed application takes about 90 days to process; a paper application takes about 10 months. The application fee is currently $35.

Trademarks

A trademark is a critical component of branding, so coming up with your company/brand name, tag line, and logo should be an integral part of your marketing processes. In Chapter 7, you'll learn how to choose a strong trademark. Here, let's focus on the legal and functional aspects of a trademark.

The United States Patent and Trademark Office (USPTO) defines a trademark as "a word, phrase, symbol, or design or a combination of words, phrases, symbols, or designs that identifies and distinguishes the source of the goods of one party from those of others." You can trademark things such as the name, slogan, and logo of your brand and/or company. For example, Nike is the trademarked name of the company and the brand; "Just Do It!" is the company's trademarked slogan; and the "Nike swoosh" (stylized checkmark) is the company's trademarked logo. In fact, these are *registered trademarks*. The trademark registration process involves making sure the trademark is available, filing an application and paying a fee to the USPTO, and waiting for the registration to be processed. Registering your mark gives you the right to put the symbol ® next to it, and it enables you to prevent or stop anyone else from using your mark for identical or related products and services.

Not all trademarks are registered. As a matter of fact, you can put the little ™ symbol next to whatever name, tag line, or logo you choose for your company—right now and for free—provided no one else in your category and/or commerce territory is using it.

Certain legal rights of ownership go with the "common-law" ™ symbol, but its main purpose is to give public notice that you claim the mark as your own and that anyone who uses or copies it could be liable for damages. If you get into a dispute with someone over who had the mark first, a judge will have to decide who was, in fact, the first user of the mark, and the other person will have to stop using it. Primarily, the ™ symbol is a cautionary sign that deters others from using your mark and establishes your use of the mark over time, which helps with branding and also when you're ready to register your trademark.

Some businesses never register their trademark. But I think it's a smart thing to do—if not before you start marketing your product, then certainly after it's been on the market for a few months and you've got some cash flowing in. Most competitors, retailers, and consumers take a registered trademark more seriously than they do a trademark. Registering a trademark usually makes it easier to prevent and stop illegal use of your mark.

Making Your Mark

Regardless of whether or when you register your trademark, you should ensure the mark is available before you start using it. If you'll be doing business only within a small geographic area, make sure no other business in that area and in your *line of commerce* (product category) is using the same mark. If you'll be doing business outside your immediate geographic area, make sure the mark is not being used by any other company in your category and in the regions you're targeting. I suggest also making sure no major national or international player is using the same or a very similar mark.

Trademark protection has two purposes: (1) to protect consumers from confusion and deception, and (2) to protect the intellectual property rights of the mark's owner. From a marketing standpoint, a trademark is also about building your brand and establishing *goodwill* in the market.

Established trademarks have considerable value. The Coca-Cola trademark, for example, is worth billions of dollars. "Any first-year chemistry student could figure out Coke's recipe using a gas chromatography machine," says John Ferrell, founding partner of Carr & Ferrell, LLP, Silicon Valley specialists in patent and intellectual property law (and my own patent attorney). "You could also just go to thisamericanlife.org and download it. But there's a perceived value associated with the Coca-Cola Company that is based on consumer experience with the brand. That value, or goodwill, is what the trademark represents."

Companies like Coca-Cola police their trademarks vigilantly. Believe me, if you infringe on the trademarks of major players, they *will* catch wind of it. You will be pursued by corporate attorneys, and you will incur costs. First, you'll have to stop using the mark. That means you will have wasted whatever money you've spent on establishing and promoting your brand, and you'll have to start all over, spending even more money and time on a new trademark. Second, you may have to pay damages.

So before you start using a trademark, you or your attorney should do a thorough search to make sure it doesn't infringe on another company's trademark. Keep in mind that the legal measure of trademark infringement is the existence or possibility of consumer confusion. Just because your mark is not exactly the same as the other company's doesn't mean it's in the clear. If your mark *sounds like*, *looks like*, or *conveys a meaning like* another company's trademark, you can't register it, and you'll be in violation of the law if you use it.

You can do a search for your own trademark on the USPTO website. To check further, you can go on a search engine such as Google, type in the name or slogan you want to trademark, and see what comes up. You can also go to a website such as Trademarkia (http://www .trademarkia.com), where you can search trademarks by name, logo, and domain. If you're a small company and only doing business in a limited geographic area, this type of search should be sufficient. Otherwise, you'll want to hire an attorney or a company that specializes in IP searches, such as Thompson & Thompson or Corsearch. Professional companies will do a more exhaustive search for you. This could be a wise choice, especially if you're spending a lot of money on promotional materials, a website, advertising, and so on. A more thorough search is also extremely important if you plan to register your trademark. Search companies have access to databases worldwide that most people don't. A typical trademark search costs from $500 to $800.

Registering Your Mark
The trademark application is fairly easy to complete and submit through the USPTO website. What can be difficult is identifying all of the categories for which you should submit your mark, doing a thorough trademark search in each of those categories, and determining whether your mark fits the criteria of "confusion" with any existing trademark. So, in most cases, I suggest hiring a trademark attorney to do the heavy lifting.

If you're seeking funding, you should register your trademarks. Lenders and investors want protection from the legal headaches and lost marketing momentum that can arise from failing to secure your place in the market with a registered trademark.

If you're self-funded and don't have the money to register your trademark(s) right away, John Ferrell suggests starting out with an unregistered trademark. "Before spending a couple thousand bucks registering a trademark, most small startups can just use the TM for a while to see whether the business is going to be successful. But as soon you start to get some traction, I'd register the mark—especially if you're a very consumer-centric company."

"Whether you're consumer-centric or not, if your mark is really important to building your brand and to sales, I'd register it as early as you possibly can. Gary Dahl, the man from Los Gatos, California, who invented the Pet Rock in 1975 knew that his trademark was much more important than the rock he was selling."

You can file the trademark registration application yourself. In the United States, the initial filing fee is currently $325 to file electronically through the Trademark Electronic Application System (TEAS). The current fee to submit a paper filing is $375. If you use a trademark attorney—which the USPTO, most attorneys, and I encourage you to do—it may cost about $1,500 or more per category. There are additional fees to pay if you file internationally. The USPTO has all filing fees listed on its website.

It typically takes six to twelve months for the USPTO to process a trademark registration application. While you're waiting for your application to be approved, use the ™ symbol.

Maintaining Your Mark

Monitor your trademark to make sure other companies and people aren't using it improperly. When someone else uses your mark, consumers can become confused and the goodwill associated with your brand can become eroded. If a lot of people repeatedly misuse or overuse your trademark over time, you risk losing your mark to dilution. For example, the word "escalator" used to be a registered trademark of the Otis Elevator Company. Then, the public started using the word generically for any brand of moving stairs: "I'm going to take the escalator." "Just use the escalator." Before long, it became so much a part of English vocabulary that it ceased to be a proper name—and Otis lost the trademark.

Another way to lose your trademark is to not use it. If you register your mark too early and it takes years to get your product to market, your right to the mark could lapse. You can also lose your mark if you've been using it steadily but then stop using it or use it very infrequently for a period of time. You have to use it continually; otherwise, someone can come in and challenge your right to the mark. In fact, if you haven't been selling the product for a while, your trademark just goes away.

If your trademark protection is not limited to a small geographic area, you not only have to continually use your mark but also continually engage in interstate commerce. That could be as simple as selling on the Internet or using interstate transportation to ship products to your distributor.

The main reason registered trademarks go out of force is because the brand has petered out or the company has gone out of business.

Patents

A patent is a legal property right granted to the person or entity that designs, invents, or cultivates a new and original product, process, technology, or service of monetary value. A patent grants the patent holder the exclusive right to make, sell, and use the idea for a specified period of time. During that time, the patent holder can sell (*assign*) the idea to another person or entity or authorize (*license*) another person or entity to manufacture, sell, or use the idea.

Patents are issued by a governing agency of the country in which the patent application is filed, and they are enforceable only in that country. In the United States, patents are issued by the USPTO.

The USPTO grants three types of patents:

- **Design patents.** This type of patent can be obtained for a reproducible change in the decorative appearance, configuration, ornamental design, or shape of a utilitarian item—for example, a change in the appearance only (not functionality) of a bottle, chair, eyeglass frame, or shovel.
- **Utility patents.** Any useful apparatus, machine, manufactured item, or composition of matter can be covered by a utility patent; the ideas of most inventor-entrepreneurs fall under this type of patent. A new manufacturing process or method of doing business can also be protected by a utility patent. Utility patents can also be granted for computer software programs and mathematical algorithms used in computer software programs. (Abstract mathematical algorithms cannot be patented.)
- **Plant patents.** This applies to a new and original species of plant that can be reproduced sexually (with seeds) or asexually (without seeds).

Some ideas require both a utility patent and a design patent. Some require two or more utility and/or design patents. We filed for an inexpensive design patent on the original shape of our Hot Picks—the skull—that defined our brand. Some people say design patents don't hold weight, but they can when shape comes into play, and the shape of our guitar picks was definitely a unique aspect of our product. Design patents are typically much less expensive than utility patents and issue much faster.

In almost every country in the world, entitlement to a patent is established on a *first-to-file* basis, meaning a patent is awarded based on the date of the application, regardless of the date of the actual invention. The United States has been the only country to grant patent protection based on a *first-to-invent* basis, meaning the patent is awarded to the first person who conceived of and "practiced" (worked on, tested, and/or produced) an invention. That changes March 16, 2013, when the new America Invents Act goes into effect and the provision changes from first to invent to first to file (see "The New America Invents Act").

THE NEW AMERICA INVENTS ACT
Gene Quinn/IPWatchdog.com

The America Invents Act (AIC) is going to change virtually everything as we know it regarding patents in the United States. The big change that's going to affect most people is switching from a first-to-invent to a first-to-file system. Although that's a huge change from a legal standpoint, it's not much of a change from a practical standpoint. If you look at the data, 99.9 percent of people who have received patents under the first-to-invent system were actually also the first to file.

The AIC includes a number of exceptions that would allow you to prevail even if you were not the first to file—for example, if you can demonstrate that you came up with the idea in the first place and someone derived their idea from yours. That's where a PPA and your inventor's logbook and other personal records will come in handy.

Under the first-to-invent system, you had 12 months from the time you first disclosed or published your invention to file a non-provisional patent. If my take on the new statute is correct, if you publish or disclose your idea and then somebody else files a patent on the same idea and it was not derived from yours, then you would be prevented from getting a patent. But we won't know how that shakes out until we start getting some case law on it.

That said, if you're following best practices—using NDAs and filing a PPA—you have nothing to worry about. Disclosure has to be public, and an NDA establishes that it's confidential. The PPA gives you 12 months of IP protection while you show and shop your idea around. The AIC will include some kind of grace period for the non-provisional patent application, but the scope of that is still unknown. So filing a PPA has always been a good idea, and it will be extremely good once the law changes to first to file.

The Power of Patent Pending

Several countries—including Australia, China, Japan, the United Kingdom, and the United States—offer *provisional patent applications* (PPAs). The U.S. version allows the inventor to obtain a *priority date* and a *patent pending* designation and corresponding number. Filing a PPA is a much simpler, faster, and less expensive process than filing a regular *nonprovisional patent application*. It is also in effect for a much shorter period of time, usually one year rather than twenty.

In the United States, PPAs apply only to ideas that fall under the utility patent category. A PPA is in force for 12 months, after which you can either file a nonprovisional patent application or let your PPA expire. If you let it expire without filing a regular patent application, you lose your original date.

A PPA is a fast, easy, affordable way to protect your intellectual property while you design and develop your idea, test the market, refine the design, figure out your manufacturing, and generate interest from potential customers.

Filing a USPTO provisional patent application provides several advantages:

- The filing fee is only $125.
- The application is simple enough that you can do it yourself, without an attorney.
- The PPA does not require the formal documentation that a regular nonprovisional patent application requires. You can submit simple drawings and even photographs of rough mock-ups.
- It provides the same legal protection as a regular patent application.
- It is in force for a period of 12 months, which is plenty of time to design and refine your idea, find a manufacturer, and test the market.
- You can include a "Patent Pending" notice on documents, drawings, sell sheets, and prototypes you present to potential manufacturers and other vendors as well as to potential customers.
- As long as the patent is pending, no potential competitor can access your patent application to rip off your idea. In fact, the USPTO won't even read your PPA until and unless you either file a regular patent application or someone disputes your rights to the idea.
- You can file multiple provisional patent applications as you work out and finalize the design within that 12-month period, before consolidating them into a single nonprovisional patent application.
- It establishes an official patent filing date for your idea. Should you decide to go for a nonprovisional patent, the filing date of your provisional patent application becomes the filing date of your regular patent, thereby extending the duration of your patent from 20 years to 21 years.

Most attorneys will not recommend a PPA. Instead, they will often want you to do a full patent application, as the process for drafting one is time-consuming, which incurs significant attorney's fees. In any case, many patent attorneys write PPAs like a regular patent application, so they will charge from $1,500 to $3,000 to do one.

You can write your own provisional patent application, but I recommend using a program like PatentWizard (http://www.patentwizard .com) from Neustel Law or PatentEase Provisional (http://www.inventor prise.com). There are other similar software applications that you can find on the Internet. You can also find inventor-friendly attorneys to review an application that you have written. The most important part of these provisional patent applications is that you include as much information as you have at the time. I'm not an attorney so I am not giving you legal advice, but I never include claims on my PPAs. Claims are required when filing for a nonprovisional patent, but they are not required on a PPA. Leaving claims off the PPA will allow you to show your application to others and keep the claims private for the time being.

In my experience, PPAs are the most powerful tools inventor-entrepreneurs can use to protect their intellectual property while bringing an idea to market. But filing a PPA should not be your first step. If you file for a PPA before you've done your market research and design work, you will have started the clock on your one year's worth of protection before you're ready to actually use it. If your research tells you the idea can't be made or isn't economically feasible or won't sell, you may not have time left to make the design workable. Then, you will have wasted the application fee and lost your original date.

Nonprovisional Patent

For many simple ideas and for certain product categories, you may never need to file for a regular nonprovisional patent. In the toy, novelty and gift, and fashion industries, for example, the market changes so rapidly and product life cycles are so short that the window of opportunity for a new product may well close before the patent even issues.

Big and highly technical ideas usually do require patent protection. Many require multiple patents, what my patent attorney, John Ferrell, calls a "wall of protection." Building a wall of protection around your intellectual property helps keep you out of court by discouraging people from copying or designing around your idea.

I'm not a patent expert, so I'll leave the details to the professionals. But here are some simple answers to the most frequently asked questions about patents:

How much does a patent cost? A utility patent costs about $8,000, including attorney's fees, though the amount can vary considerably. A design patent costs less. Keep in mind that most ideas require more than one patent, and a price tag from $10,000 to $20,000 for utility patent(s) for a single idea is not at all unusual.

How long does it take for a patent to issue? Each patent application is reviewed by a patent examiner. From my experiences, this process can take up to 36 months, sometimes even longer. Rarely is a patent granted immediately upon the initial examination. Typically, the examiner comes back to the patent applicant with *office actions*—questions and requests for additional information, drawings, documentation, or other clarification. In fact, the patent examination process usually consists of two or more rounds of office actions followed by a waiting period for a response.

After all of that, which can easily take four years, the examiner may reject some of the claims in the patent or reject the patent application outright. You then have the option of filing a request for reconsideration or an appeal, which prolongs the process even further. The patent process can easily go on three to four years and still not result in a patent being issued.

How long is a patent valid? A design patent protects IP rights for a period of 14 years from the date the patent is *granted*. Utility patents (the most common type) and plant patents protect IP rights for a period of 20 years from the date the patent is *filed*. A utility patent, unlike design and plant patents, requires the patent holder to pay a maintenance fee at 3½ years, 7½ years, and 11½ years. The amount of the maintenance fee depends on whether your company has fewer or more than 500 employees, with smaller companies paying a lower fee. Failure to pay a maintenance fee results in the termination of the patent.

Do I need an attorney to file a patent? Whether an idea is complicated or simple, filing and defending a patent takes a lot of time, money, and expertise. I would not even consider filing a nonprovisional patent application myself! I strongly advise you as an inventor-entrepreneur to retain the services of a good patent attorney or patent agent if and when you decide to try to patent your idea.

Working with an Attorney

Before you call a patent or IP attorney or patent agent, do what is necessary to have a basic understanding of the laws and processes applying to nonprovisional patents, PPAs, trademarks, or copyrights. Don't call an attorney with questions for which you can easily find the answers for free through the USPTO website, books, and articles and blogs written by patent experts. Attorneys are expensive, and you pay for every hour they spend and every task they perform on your behalf.

A patent attorney is only as good as the information you provide him or her. The attorney's job is to clearly and completely document your invention in the language and format appropriate for the patent application process, not to solve your design or manufacturing problems. So, before you contact an attorney, it's important for you to know your idea inside and out, every aspect of its design; how it will be manufactured, what materials will be used; unique (patentable) features. I also suggest you do a *prior art search* to determine whether any patents relating to your invention already exist and what the differences are between those ideas and yours.

Prior art for a patent application means anything published before the filing date of the patent, which describes the same or similar invention. You can go to USPTO and learn how to conduct a review of prior art. I prefer using a search engine such as Google Patent; a search engine that indexes patent and patent applications from the USPTO. You can also use an independent third party to do your search, which you can find on the Internet. I would advise against using your own patent attorney. In my opinion, doing so would be a conflict of interest. I also recommend trying to do some of the searching yourself because with a little experience, you can get pretty good at this and save money.

Make sure your inventor's logbook is up-to-date and complete. Create any additional documentation and drawings you may need to fully describe your idea. If you have a prototype, get one for your attorney. If your lawyer can see and touch it, he or she will better know how to talk about your product. I've learned from experience that without a prototype, some attorneys just won't get it.

When you're ready to hire a patent attorney, don't just pick one out of the phone directory. The best way to find an attorney is to get a referral, preferably from another inventor who has patented an idea in your category. The USPTO has a huge list of patent attorneys on its site; so does the American Bar Association (ABA). In fact, make sure the attorney you're considering is listed with USPTO and is a member in good standing of the ABA. Find someone you feel comfortable with and trust who specializes in patent law and has experience with your product category or industry. Read patents that he or she has written. A well-written patent should be understandable to everyone. If you can't understand a patent, it's not well written.

Meet with the attorney and get a written price quote before signing a retainer. Most patent attorneys will meet with you briefly for free or for a small fixed fee. During that initial meeting, get a breakdown of what the attorney will do for you. Ask how he or she bills: Hourly? Every 15 minutes? By the minute? Make sure the attorney understands the nature of your idea. Different inventions need different amounts of time and work. If your idea is simple, you shouldn't be charged for a complicated one. Question whether the attorney charges extra for office actions, and if so, by how much. Find out if there's anything you can do to reduce expenses. Talk about what might happen if attorney's fees go over the quote; up to a 10 percent overage is acceptable.

Strategize with your attorney on how best to protect your idea. A good patent attorney can help you expand the scope of your patent to build a necessary wall of protection around your idea, but you will need to figure out all the ways a competitor may try to get around you. Do the homework to identify each way your idea could be used, made, and improved upon, and then provide that information to your patent attorney so he or she can include all those possible design and manufacturing variations in your patent applications.

Have the attorney draft the claims first. Make sure you understand and agree with how the claims are written before moving on to the rest of the process. Finally, don't phone your attorney about every little thing, and don't make small talk! It's too expensive. Send brief e-mails, and be efficient with the attorney's time. Get everything in writing, and take notes so you won't forget what you've talked about.

• • •

Using these strategies—including or excluding patenting your product—will help you prevent and overcome the most common threats to your idea and your company. It will give you the protection you need and the peace of mind you want as you launch your business, bring your product to market, and build your brand.

Ready, Set, Launch!

WHEN YOU'VE come up with an idea you're so passionate about that you want to build a business around, it can be very tempting to start spending money to give your new company the appearance and accoutrements of a big-time player. But, most of the time, it's both unnecessary and unwise to start out big—with a fancy office, a bunch of employees, and a big overhead budget. That kind of spending is *never* a good idea if it means going into debt.

Of course, it is important to look and act like a "real" business, and there are certain things you must have and do to get your business up and running. But you can do that at a much lower cost and risk than many people realize.

No MBA? No Problem!

A lot of first-time inventor-entrepreneurs feel inadequate by not having a résumé loaded with impressive credentials. Guess what? Many very successful entrepreneurs have little or no formal education and prior experience in business.

I don't have a master's degree. When I married Janice, I was impressed with how well educated she is. She has a bachelor's degree in political science from Stanford University and a master's degree in marketing from Northwestern. When she worked for E&J Gallo Winery, everyone I met there had an MBA as well. I felt out of place when I would join Janice at company social functions. It took me a while to realize I belonged at that table as much as anyone else did—and that I had something they didn't. Each of those people worked on a specific aspect of the business, but none had the ultimate responsibility for the company's success or failure because, unlike me, they didn't own the business.

Being an entrepreneur isn't about having an MBA; it's about having passion. I didn't see that entrepreneurial passion in many of the people I met at Gallo.

I don't think you need an MBA to be a successful entrepreneur. Having a lot of information isn't the same thing as actually doing something with it. You can learn and accomplish a lot by educating yourself, studying the market, and just getting out there and doing it. Even some of the top MBA programs in the country are now emphasizing the need for real-world information and concrete action over theory when starting a business!

One thing I think you do need to have is common sense. Not long ago, I was a guest lecturer at an MBA program and sat in on a class. A lot of brilliant people were in attendance, most in their late twenties or early thirties, and I was amazed by the comments and questions from the class. They were all about facts and figures, things they had learned from case studies, but they had no practical knowledge and lacked common sense. They might have known how to write a dazzling 50-page business plan, but they had no idea how to make a great presentation to a potential investor or customer. They didn't realize that if you don't grab your audience's attention and wow them in the first 30 seconds, those people are never going to look at your business plan.

So, if you're worried about not having fancy business credentials, remember this: an elite résumé is optional. Passion, common sense, and practical experience are invaluable.

Now, let's look at some smart ways to get the information and help you need to launch and soar.

Free Advice and Assistance

Get as much free advice and assistance as you can from as many people and resources as you can. Definitely run your business concept and questions by your mentors and anyone you know who has hands-on experience in whatever it is you need. One of the best advisors and allies you can have is another inventor-entrepreneur who has a business similar to yours. Another great resource is an older or retired entrepreneur or business executive. Some people may be willing to help you, at little or no cost, with certain aspects of starting up your company, such as setting up your accounting systems or writing your business plan. One way to find those individuals in the United States is through the Small Business Association *S*ervice *C*orps *of R*etired *E*xecutives (SCORE), which has regional offices throughout the country. Trade shows, trade organizations, trade magazines, and social media networks are other ways of finding senior professionals with success under their belts who might be willing to share their expertise.

The Small Business Administration (SBA) offers counseling, training, and assistance programs to small businesses, including specialized programs for veterans and women. Although the SBA has helped a lot of people, be aware that many of its counselors and instructors have limited knowledge. So don't rely only on their advice; always talk with people who have actually started and owned a successful business.

Every community, state, and country has various government agencies, nonprofit organizations, and membership associations that support entrepreneurs and small businesses. Most also have organizations and clubs for specific segments of the population (such as African Americans or women) and specific types of businesses or industries. There are also entrepreneurship nonprofit organizations with a global reach.

Local colleges, universities, and trade schools are another fantastic resource not only for free information but also for free and low-cost goods and services, such as market research, engineering drawings, prototypes, and graphic design. Most community colleges also offer low-cost business courses designed specifically for small business owners and entrepreneurs.

Bartering

Bartering is the exchange of goods and/or services between independent contractors or companies. U.S. businesses barter more than $30 billion worth of goods and services every year. More than one-third of small businesses and some of the largest corporations in the world engage in bartering.

"Fortune 500 companies barter all the time," says Kedma Ough, who runs the Micro-Inventor's Program of Oregon (a nonprofit organization that helps inventors bring new technology and innovation to market) as well as a consulting firm she founded to help small businesses thrive, AVITA (http://www.avitabiz.com/), both of which operate nationwide.

Kedma suggests using a commercial or nonprofit barter exchange (or trade exchange) organization that acts as a broker and record-keeper for all participating members. These programs are based on a point system, where every service or product that is traded has a value. The bartering agency records every transaction and keeps track of all the points contributed and cashed in by each member. At the end of the year, each member gets a report of all the bartering he or she has done, for tax purposes.

There are thousands of business barter exchanges out there. Two that Kedma recommends are the National Association of Trade Exchanges (NATE; http://www.natebarter.com) and International Reciprocal Trade Association (IRTA; http://www.irta.com).

You can also barter directly with another company or professional. With Hot Picks, for example, we gave guitar picks to some magazines in exchange for advertising space. With direct barters, make sure you use a written barter agreement that specifies the value of the goods or services exchanged, both yours and the other party's.

It's also a good idea to have whomever you're bartering with sign a confidentiality agreement. If you barter, check with your tax accountant to see whether you need to file a Form 1099-B (Proceeds from Broker and Barter Exchange Transactions) or a Form 1099-MISC with your tax returns.

Among the many things that can be bartered are bookkeeping services, office space, office furnishings and equipment, tax preparation, logo design, business cards, secretarial services, computer maintenance and repair, market research, and prototype fabrication. As long as both parties come to an agreement, anything can be bartered, and the items exchanged do not need to be of equal value.

Outsourcing

You're probably going to need and will want help with certain projects and certain aspects of your business, but you don't need to hire employees right off the bat. At Hot Picks, I often used my family and friends as my workforce. When my wife and kids helped pack our guitar picks into their clamshell containers, we called it a "pick party." Of course, the company paid them, but the cost of their service was a lot cheaper than the cost of using outside help.

Another option is to *outsource*—which is simply hiring a person or company to do something for you on a freelance, or contractual, basis. You can outsource everything from building your prototype to designing your logo, doing your bookkeeping, and filling customer orders.

The more experienced the contractor or bigger the company, the more you can expect to pay for the services. If you were to outsource everything to top-notch pros, it could quickly add up to a lot of money. A smarter approach is to find less experienced professionals and smaller companies that can give you good service at a better price.

A great way to outsource on a shoestring is to call a technical school or college professor and ask if any students or recent graduates are available who are outstanding in whatever you need help with. Online outsourcing networks such as Elance (http://elance.com) and Guru (http://www.guru.com) give you access to independent contractors around the world, including in your own community.

Do You Need a Business Plan?

If you were to ask 100 small business owners if they had written a business plan when they first started their company, probably 90 of them would say no. Many never write a business plan. Those who do write one at the beginning usually do so in order to get outside funding. Those who write one later often do so because their business is in trouble or they want to sell it. Most will claim they didn't write a business plan because they didn't need one, and there is probably some truth to that. But I suspect many don't write one because they don't know how to do so and are intimidated by the complexity of traditional business plans.

When we started Hot Picks, the last thing on my mind was creating a business plan. I'd heard about them, of course. But when I read some examples, I didn't know half of what was being talked about. It seemed too complicated.

What I didn't realize then but do now is that all the homework and analyses I was doing to determine whether to move forward with my idea—who would buy it, how much they would pay for it, its unique benefit, how to manufacture and distribute it, how much it would cost, how much profit I would make—are all part of business planning. Even the sales sheets I was creating to highlight the benefits of my ideas involved thinking and verbiage that go into a business plan.

Once Hot Picks was up and running, I did write a business plan. It helped us to project revenues, expenses, and profits; to manage our cash flow and inventory; to respond to large orders, such as from Walmart; and to prioritize and focus on building our brand and business. But our business plan was much shorter and simpler than the kind big companies create, business schools teach, and many experts recommend.

I'm still not convinced you need a long, involved business plan for a small business and a simple idea, especially when you first start up and if you're self-funded. For one thing, those kinds of business plans are based on a lot of assumptions. I want real information and real results—the kind of data I get from studying and testing the market, talking with potential vendors and customers, and doing the math.

That said, I think it is important to write a short, focused business plan when you first start your business. If you find you need a more comprehensive business plan—for a grant, loan, investor, or whatever—you can use your one-page plan as the executive summary and build from there. Later, as your company changes and grows, you can update and change your plan to whatever format and scope you need.

Since I am not an expert in developing business plans, I asked someone who is to weigh in on the subject: Jim Horan, author of the bestselling book *One Page Business Plan* and founder/CEO of One Page Business Plan Company. I had the pleasure of interviewing Jim, which gave me better insight as to his approach in creating a great one-page business plan. The following are Jim's thoughts and advice about business plans for small business startups.

Why Every Startup Needs a Simple Business Plan

Inventor-entrepreneurs tend to be highly creative people who lock in on their idea, determine who it's for, and figure out how they're going to distribute it . . . and then giddy-up and go! That might work up to a point—until they run into trouble, or bring on a partner, or need to raise or borrow money. Then, just talking about the business isn't good enough. You need a business plan. A business plan is also helpful when you're seeking feedback about the viability of your business concept and in managing your business on a day-to-day basis.

Business is extraordinarily complex, even a one-person business. So you need a business plan, in whatever format it happens to be, to organize and articulate what you're doing, how you're doing it, and why. What a business plan really represents is a set of informed decisions based on your best thinking about your business.

As a consultant to small and midsize businesses and lifestyle entrepreneurs, Jim discovered a few things: Business owners love to talk about their businesses, and most talk in sound bites. Although most had never written down a plan, the key phrases and facts they were telling him added up, essentially, to their business plans. They just needed help getting those key phrases and facts down on paper.

Another thing Jim realized is that it's very difficult for small startups to accurately predict revenues, expenses, and so forth. He also kept running into entrepreneurs and business owners who had built the wrong business because they had never developed a blueprint for growth. Instead, they were opportunistic and kept bolting products and services onto their business. Consequently, they were always running out of cash and not achieving the profitability they'd hoped for. It occurred to Jim that if you can't describe what you're doing, you'll probably build the wrong business and probably never get the numbers right.

As a result of those experiences, Jim developed the One Page Business Plan to provide entrepreneurs and small business owners with a tool to help them come up with the right words and the right numbers to chart their company's course.

The One Page Business Plan

Jim Horan's One Page Business Plan™ consists of five elements. The objective is to capture the most critical elements of your plan in as few words as possible. While it's often easier to start by creating your vision statement and working your way down to your action plans, you can start with whatever element you want and complete the other elements in any order.

1. **Vision statement.** Answer the question, *What are you building?* Describe the business you are building in one to three short sentences. Your vision statement should reflect a three- to five-year horizon and include the geographic scope of your business, type of business, core products, and profile of your ideal customer.
2. **Mission statement.** Answer the question, *Why does this business exist?* Describe who your business serves (the target market) and how they will benefit from your product. A well-crafted mission statement should be 8 to 12 words long and memorable.
3. **Objectives.** Answer the compound question, *How do you define success, and what business results must you measure?* List up to nine short, one-sentence objectives. Typical objectives include sales, profit before tax, gross margin, number of customers or transactions, average sale, and other key operational goals. Defining your objectives makes it easier to allocate your time, cash, and critical resources to the things that will actually grow your business.
4. **Strategies.** Answer the question, *What will make this business successful over time?* Describe how you intend to build and grow your business. In essence, your strategies are your recipe for suc-

cess. List up to nine critical things you must consistently do well over time—for example, marketing outreach, initial trial, pricing, closing, product/service quality, and customer service.

5. **Action plans.** Answer the question, *What work needs to be done?* Describe the major business-building steps, projects, and programs that must be undertaken to implement your strategies and achieve your objectives. Identify four to nine major projects or programs to be undertaken over the planning period (usually one year), and specify when each will be achieved.

Here is a simple, powerful visual technique to help you craft your action plans:

1. Draw a large circle on a piece of paper.
2. Draw two lines, one from top to bottom and one from side to side, so that the circle is divided into four equal parts. Each part represents a quarter of the year.
3. In each quarter, write down the one or two projects/programs you plan to complete during that three-month period (for example, January through March).

This One Page Planning Wheel™ spells out your one-year action plan on a single page.

Show Me the Money!

When you're starting a business, these are usually the first things on your mind: How will I get the money? Should I sell my house and cash in my retirement? Should I ask my family and friends to chip in? Should I borrow it? Look for investors?

Frankly, coming up with enough cash to launch your business and keep it going until you've got enough positive cash flow is one of the toughest areas for most people. It helps to start with a business plan that answers the critical question: how much money do I need? It also helps to make a budget and stick with it. I also suggest saving money and not quitting your day job. Even when a launch goes great, it usually takes a while before a new small business starts earning a profit. So, if you have a job, you might want to hold on to it and work on your own business "on the side," at least initially. Be frugal, too, not only with your business expenditures but also with your personal spending. The more money you save, the farther your money will go.

If you follow the approach outlined in this book—starting small and with a simple idea, testing your idea before spending a dime, and being frugal—you won't need a lot of money to get your business up and running. But at some point, you're going to have to start spending some cash, whether to cover startup expenses, operating expenses, or both.

There are many ways to come up with those funds. The best ways, in my opinion, are to use your own money and get whatever "free" money you can. So I encourage you to start there and then explore other funding options only if and when absolutely necessary.

Self-Funding

When you have "skin in the game," as billionaire businessman Warren Buffett famously refers to using your own money, you tend to work harder to keep it. You don't spend as freely, and you tend to control your money. When you borrow money or start bringing on partners, investors, or stockholders, there's a lot of pressure. I don't like that type of pressure.

Here are some potential sources for self-funding your business:

- **Savings accounts.** Withdrawing from your savings is probably the least risky way to fund your business.
- **Profit-sharing plans, 401(k)s, IRAs, and pension plans.** If you have any of these accounts, check to see whether you can pull money out and how much you can take. You may have to pay a penalty for doing so. This isn't my first choice for a way to fund a business, but in my opinion, it's better than going into debt. I know a lot of financial planners would disagree, but I just really hate owing people money.
- **Life insurance.** See if you can borrow against your life insurance.

- **Stocks, bonds, and other financial assets.** If you own stocks or bonds, you might consider liquidating them to invest in your own company.
- **Luxury assets.** Sell vacation or second homes, investment property, extra cars, recreational vehicles, valuable artwork, jewelry, gold and silver, or other possessions you feel comfortable parting with.

Although I'm a big fan of self-financing, I don't think it's a good idea to liquidate all of your assets and to drain your savings, retirement, and children's education funds for your business. Before you dig too deeply into those resources, explore other sources of "free" money, such as grants and no-repay loans. You may also want to consult with a financial planner before you start pulling money out of your accounts or selling off your assets.

Family, Friends, and Others

Many entrepreneurs get at least some startup funding from people they know, commonly known as "family, friends, and others" (FFO). Sometimes, an FFO with the resources to do so will give you the money as a gift you don't have to repay, so you probably should avail yourself of this when you can. Sometimes, FFO funds come as a no-interest or low-interest loan, or with a delayed payment schedule. Other times, the FFO will want to become a shareholder in the company.

My advice is to use this financing option as a last resort. It's one thing to risk my own money. It's worse to risk someone else's—especially a family member's or friend's.

Crowdfunding

Crowdfunding is when a large group of people individually contribute small amounts of money to an entrepreneur, inventor, startup, or small business. Receiving a lot of small monetary "gifts" ($25, $100, $500, $1,000, up to $20,000) from family, friends, and others to help fund or grow your business is one form of crowdfunding. A relatively new form gaining in popularity is online crowdfunding companies that serve as intermediaries (essentially, brokers) between people trying to raise capital for their projects or enterprises and people who want to contribute funds to those projects and enterprises.

Some crowdfunding platforms allow you to raise money for startup or growth capital. Many allow only project-based crowdfunding. Of course, that "project" can be anything from building a prototype to creating a website, creating a promotional campaign, increasing inventory, or another initiative. Typically, you set your funding goal (the minimum amount of money you want or need to raise) and your timeline for reaching it (for example, 30 days). If you do not reach your minimum funding goal within that time period, you collect no money. Only if you meet or exceed your funding goal within that time period do you collect the funds—minus the site's commission (3 to 5 percent) and payment processing fee (3 to 4 percent).

There are two types of crowdfunding companies: those offering nonequity funding and those offering equity funding.

Nonequity Crowdfunding

Nonequity funding means the funders or backers give you money as a gift. They don't become shareholders in your company, and you don't pay back the money. As a bonus, some funders are successful entrepreneurs who offer valuable feedback to the recipient of their crowdfunding pledge, which can be up to $10,000.

Some popular nonequity crowdfunding sites include:

IndieGogo.com: for creative, "cause" (nonprofit), and entrepreneurial projects
Kickstarter.com: for creative projects—fashion, product design, technology, etc.
FundaGeek.com: for technical and scientific inventions
Peerbackers.com: for entrepreneurs, inventors, and "trailblazers"

As a recipient of the funding, you are expected to give each funder a "reward" for his or her donation—if and when your goal is reached and you actually receive funding. A reward is basically a thank-you gift. Most recipients offer different rewards for different levels of funding; the higher the donation, the better the reward. The best rewards are fun or useful to the funder and promote your business—such as cups, pens, decals, and t-shirts bearing your logo and tag line, and, for bigger donations, your product.

Equity Crowdfunding

With equity-based crowdfunding, funders are considered small-stake investors who become shareholders in your company. In other words, they each get a tiny slice of your pie.

In April 2012, the U.S. Congress voted in the JOBS (Jumpstart Our Business Startups) Act, making way for equity-based crowdfunding platforms in which individuals can invest small amounts of money in startups and early-stage businesses. Now any U.S. citizen can donate or invest up to $10,000 of his or her personal money to a private U.S. company each year, and a U.S. company can receive up to $1 million in small-stake investment funds per year or up to $2 million if all investors are provided with audited financial statements (per specifications of the Securities and Exchange Commission, or SEC).

Just remember: every small-stake investor owns a piece of your company, entitling the investor to that percentage of your profits—including any profit from the sale of your company. The more investors you have, the more difficult it is to manage and stretch your profits. It can also make it next to impossible to secure angel investors or venture capital later.

Partners

You could bring on partners. I had a partner with Hot Picks, Rob Stephani, and each of us put in money. We made sure we had the same goals and that our skill sets did not overlap. We formed a limited liability company or (LLC). We were owner-managers, meaning we owned the company and ran the company together. Our partnership gave us the workforce we needed to be successful. Having a partner can get complicated. The relationship doesn't always work, but it worked for us.

Grants

A grant is an award, or gift, of money from a government agency, non-profit organization, or corporation. The best thing about a grant is that you don't have to pay it back or exchange anything for it. You just have to show that you need the money and how you will put it to good use in your business. Grant money is available to help with startup costs and other things, to enable you to do something you'd planned to do anyway (e.g., hiring an employee or buying equipment), or to help you grow your business (e.g., to initiate a project or program to increase sales or improve profit margins). A grant may also take the form of goods (e.g., a computer) or services (e.g., consulting).

Finding a Grant
There are thousands of grants available to inventors, entrepreneurs, and small businesses, with awards ranging from $1,000 to $750,000. According to Kedma Ough, the challenge is to find the right grant(s) for you.

"You don't want to spend your time and energy going after grants you'll never get," advises Kedma. "Research and target your grants just like you would your market."

She suggests starting by searching for grants for a specific demographic that applies to you. For example, if you're a veteran, you could search the Internet with the key words "business grants veterans." If you're disabled, search under "disabled" and then the specific disability, for example, "blind." If you're a woman, search "women entrepreneurs" and "small business owners." One such grant is Count Me In (http://www.countmein.org), which grants awards to women-owned businesses that want to grow to more than $1 million. If you're a minority, search under that minority group. For example, the Alaska Native American Competition awards $100,000 in grants to the winning small business owners.

Next, search for inventor, entrepreneur, and small business grants from various federal, state, and local government agencies and nonprofit organizations. "For example, if I were looking for grants for a small business in Portland, Oregon, there is a city program that gives you 50 percent of the cost, up to $5,000, to train someone you hire," Kedma says.

One $2.2 billion federally funded and administered program is the U.S. Small Business Innovation Research (SBIR) / Small Business Technology Transfer Reauthorization (STTR) program. The SBIR/ STTR program provides contracts and grants to businesses to help move and cluster technology throughout the country. The idea or business can be for new technology you've created or for existing technology you've applied in an innovative way.

You might also want to search by "urban" or "rural" or for your type of business, product category, industry, or specialized focus (such as "green" business). For example, the MillerCoors Urban Entrepreneur Series (MUES) business plan competition, though designed for minority entrepreneurs, is open to anyone over the age of 21 who is starting a small business or owns a small to midsize business that is fewer than five years old. "What they care about is you giving them good ideas and putting together a fun business plan that fits into the scope of their enterprise," Kedma says. MUES grants one $50,000 award and up to four $25,000 awards each year.

"The more specific you are in your search, the closer you'll be to getting the grants you need," Kedma says.

Applying for Grants

Most grant applications consist of or include a written grant proposal, the requirements for which vary from grant to grant. You can learn the ins and outs of grant writing from books, self-help tutorials, and community college courses. You can also use templates. You will need to tailor each proposal to the grant you're applying for.

Many grant applications call for a business plan and certain financial documents, such as cash-flow projections, income statements, and balance sheets. In some cases, a one-page business plan or executive summary may be enough. In other cases, a more comprehensive business plan may be required. A MUES grant, for example, requires a 15- to 30-page business plan.

FUNDING BUZZY
Amy Baxter/Buzzy4shots

The SBIR grant we applied for, through the National Institutes of Health and the National Science Foundation, is called a Fast Track. I wouldn't recommend anybody doing that, because the odds of getting one are small. But we were too naïve to know that, so we applied for a proof-of-concept grant and received approximately $180,000. Then, after doing the R&D, prototyping, and testing, we got the remainder of the grant, about $1.1 million, to do a full-scale, rigorous, randomized-control trial. That grant application was about 200 pages and took three solid months of writing and revising.

The grant was rejected the first time. So I got some help from a Georgia business development group that is trying to help local small businesses, and a woman named Julie Collins looked at our grant application pro bono. She suggested putting my product in a different product category, which we did. In that arena, our simple little vibrating thing with a cold pack was novel enough that they understood the need for it, and we got the grant.

Credit

A lot of people use credit cards to fund their businesses, but you have only 30 days before interest starts. You can get into trouble quickly. If you're going to use credit cards, shop around to get the lowest interest rate possible, try not to max them out, and try to pay off the balance each month.

Getting a small business or startup loan from a bank is nearly impossible. The only time a bank lends money is when you don't need it! Some entrepreneurs get unsecured personal loans or secure a loan with their personal assets (for example, a second mortgage or home equity line of credit). I think that's a bad idea.

Low-interest, no-collateral microloans are available to small businesses in some countries. The only microloan program I'm aware of in the United States is run by the Small Business Administration, but borrowers do pay interest and usually need to put up collateral (equipment, property, inventory). The lenders are private, nonprofit intermediaries. Loan amounts range from $100 to $35,000, and the maximum term is six years. The average SBA microloan is $10,500, and the loan is for a period of 42 months. This type of loan is hard to get, and the collateral and interest involved make me uneasy.

Only slightly better are guaranteed loans and forgivable loans.

With a guaranteed loan, a government agency (either local, state, or federal) essentially underwrites a percentage of a loan you obtain from a bank or commercial lending institution (such as a credit union). You are responsible for repaying the loan, with interest, unless you default on the loan as a consequence of your business failing. Only then does the government agency pay the lender the guaranteed portion of the debt. The Small Business Administration, for example, guarantees up to 80 percent of loans up to $1 million (principal) and with a term of up to 10 years for "established small businesses capable of repaying a loan from cash flow, but whose principals may be looking for a longer term to reduce payments or may have inadequate corporate or personal assets to collateralize the loan." Of course, that's of no help to startups, and SBA-guaranteed loans are very hard to get.

Forgivable loans are another possible funding option, but they can be tricky. A forgivable loan is when a government agency or nonprofit organization lends you money for your business that you don't have to repay . . . *if* you meet certain requirements. For example, the loan may be interest-free and forgivable only if you contribute $2 of your own money for every $1 you borrow, the loan is for no more than 50 percent of the cost of the project being financed, your business is located in a specific area, and you stay in business for five years.

The only form of credit I'm really comfortable with is getting a little extra time to pay a vendor. Vendors usually give you 30 days to pay their invoices. You can ask your vendors to extend your credit— say, to 45, 60, or 90 days. This gives you more time to sell the product and get some cash coming in. But I wouldn't ask for extended credit on the first or second order; I'd wait until you've had at least a few positive transactions with the vendor first.

Angels and Sharks

An angel investor is a wealthy individual (or group of wealthy individuals) who invests his or her own money in a private company. A venture capitalist is an individual or firm that manages an investment fund of pooled money from different sources (which may be individuals, companies, or both). Angels and venture capitalists invest money in a company in exchange for either convertible debt or an equity interest in the company—in other words, they get a piece of your pie.

Investors are rarely interested in small startups and early-stage businesses. Having investors is complicated and risky. I like to keep things simple, and I don't like risk. I've never had investors, and I don't intend to have them.

If you go after investors, you'll need to have a business valuation, a comprehensive business plan, and a slew of financial documents. You will need to provide proof of concept and a prototype, and you'll probably need to have had some sales or at least substantial advance orders.

Angels tend to be interested in startups and early-stage companies that have high growth potential. Their investments typically range from $25,000 to $2 million, and they expect a return on investment that is 3 to 10 times the amount they put in. Angels often want a seat on your board of directors.

Venture capitalists are only interested in established businesses with a proven track record and extremely high growth potential. They may invest $1 million, $10 million, $100 million, or more. Venture capitalists want a return on investment (ROI) of 5 to 10 times their investment, and they demand complete transparency. When venture capitalists have a stake in your company, they take it very seriously and have a big say in your business. That's why I call them sharks.

Setting Up Your Business

When I first envisioned what it would mean to own my own business, I imagined this nice office with new furniture. It's true that presentation is important to your branding; how people perceive your business will affect how they treat it. But when you're first starting out, you don't need to buy or rent office and warehouse space, and you definitely don't need nice furniture. You can set up your business, do everything you need to do, and cultivate an air of legitimacy without spending a lot of time and money.

Your Business Identity

Your business can be as small and simple as you want or need it to be. You can be a one-person operation and work at home in your pajamas, at least in the beginning. But anything you present to customers, vendors, retailers, the media, at trade shows, and so on must make a positive and professional impression. That includes your *business identity*, which typically consists of your company/brand name, logo, and slogan—basically, your trademarks. It may also include certain colors and images you've chosen for your brand. You don't need to have all of that in place when you first start, but you do need at least your company name. Since your business identity is a critical component of your brand, you need to create a strong brand identity; Chapter 7 discusses creating brand identity.

Although you are not required to register your trademarks with the United States Patent and Trademark Office, it is a good idea to do so (see Chapter 4). You also will probably need to register your business name with your local government agency. In some states, such as California, if you use your last name in your business name you do not need to file a fictitious "doing business as" (DBA) name, which would save money.

Your Work Space

Many inventor-entrepreneurs start off working out of their homes, garages, or basements so they don't have to pay rent. In fact, all seven of the inventor-entrepreneurs who have contributed to this book work out of their home, although a few are quickly outgrowing that space.

Some new small business owners rent small offices that are slightly off the beaten path and/or share office space with other businesses to minimize overhead costs.

If you're using a bedroom as your office and half of your garage as a warehouse, don't use those spaces for anything else (such as a guest bedroom and storage space for personal items). Things will run much more smoothly, and you'll be able to claim the workspace as a deduction on your tax returns. You will need a dedicated business address, but if you work out of your home, you can just reserve a post office box for that purpose.

If you can't or don't want to work out of your home, consider renting a small office. Read your lease agreement carefully, and know what you can and can't do. A lot of office buildings want you to sign a two- or three-year lease, which is not necessarily a bad idea, but a month-to-month lease may be better until you get your feet on the ground. I would not sign a lease for more than three years.

Move to a bigger space only when you have to because you've outgrown your space. When you do reach that point, consider purchasing rather than leasing it. Some local government agencies offer grants to small businesses to purchase property for their business.

ROUGHIN' IT AND LOVIN' IT
David Mayer/Clean Bottle

I tell people, "You're not really a grassroots company unless you actually have grass roots growing into your product because it's outside on your lawn." That's because half of my products are inside my garage; the other half are outside my garage. Our worldwide headquarters is run out of one of the bedrooms of my house. I've got two recent college grads working for me out of their homes.

Furnishings, Equipment, and Technology

Don't go out and spend money you haven't made on office furnishings. Buy used stuff, or repurpose what you already have.

You definitely will need a computer with high-speed Internet access, a printer, and a fax. These days, every business needs a website.

Since your website is your online calling card and an important part of your marketing (and sales), having a well-designed website is essential; that topic is discussed in Chapter 7.

You should also have a dedicated phone line with voicemail capabilities. You can use a mobile phone as your dedicated line. At some point, depending on how many incoming and outgoing calls you have, you may need to expand your communication capabilities (e.g., setting up a virtual PBX system) or outsource to a call center. A 24-hour answering service is nice, but it may not be worth the cost at first; as long as you have a reliable voicemail system and respond to messages quickly, you should be fine. When setting up your initial phone service, find out whether you can scale up your phone system later, either by upgrading the existing service or porting your number to a new carrier. You may also want to install Skype on your computer or smart phone.

No matter what, keep your original phone number! You can add phone numbers, but never change your original phone number or your e-mail address. One sure way to lose contact with customers is to change your contact information.

Think carefully before getting a toll-free number for your business because you will pay for each incoming call. If you get a lot of long-distance calls from customers, having a toll-free number might be worth it, because some people will hesitate to make a long-distance call or a call to an area code they don't recognize. Toll-free numbers also give you a record of every call that comes in.

Set Up Your Business Entity

For tax and legal purposes, you'll need to set up your company as a sole proprietorship, limited partnership, limited liability company (LLC), C corporation, or S corporation. You may find that your business qualifies for more than one type of business structure, in which case you'll need to decide which structure is best for you. For example, one of the advantages of becoming a limited liability company or a corporation, rather than a sole proprietorship or limited partnership, is that it protects your personal assets. Figuring out how to structure your business and filing all the paperwork is beyond the capability of most small business owners. So I suggest consulting with a SCORE volunteer or hiring an accountant or attorney to set up your business entity for you.

Licenses and Permits

One of the first things you're going to need to do is get a business license from your city. If you work out of your home, check with the city to find out whether you need any other permits and if the type of business you are running from your home is allowed in a residential area. Running a business from your home typically isn't a problem; however, if there is too much traffic in and out of the house during the day, it could be an issue for people living nearby. You probably won't have too many people coming by in the beginning, but it's best to know of potential problems before they arise.

Tax Identification

If you are a U.S. citizen and your business is a sole proprietorship, you can use your social security number for tax purposes. For all other types of businesses, you'll have to obtain an employer identification number (EIN).

Insurance

You'll need to purchase product liability and general liability insurance, which are not that expensive. Depending on the nature and activities of your particular business, state law may require that your business be covered by different or additional forms of insurance, such as professional liability, commercial property, or home-based business insurance.

Some people mistakenly think that structuring your business as a limited liability company or corporation limits the need for business liability insurance. Although these business structures do protect the personal assets of the owner from business liabilities, it is unwise to rely on business structure as a substitute for liability insurance, which covers your business from losses.

If you have employees, you are required by state law to pay certain types of insurance, the most common being workers' compensation insurance, unemployment insurance (a tax), and disability insurance.

Contact your insurance agent or broker to see if you can get this type of insurance through him or her; if not, find an agent or broker who does carry insurance for businesses.

Banking, Bookkeeping, and Record-Keeping

Setting up a business checking account is a must. You don't want to mix your personal banking with your business banking. Don't use your personal credit card for business expenses, either; instead, get a credit card for your business, and use it only for business expenses.

If you want to accept credit cards and electronic payments from customers, you'll need to set up a merchant account with your bank. If you'll be buying and/or selling goods or services online, you'll need to set up a PayPal (or similar) account.

You can outsource your bookkeeping and accounting, rather than hiring a part-time or full-time employee to perform those functions. Of course, you'll need to learn the basics so that you can oversee those processes. Another option is to do at least some of your bookkeeping yourself using a computer software program such as Quicken. If you take that approach, I suggest you hire a bookkeeper or accountant to help you set up your books and get you up to speed on how to use them.

● ● ●

Starting a business doesn't have to wipe you out. You can save up some money before you start spending, and you can finance your business with your own money and donated funds you don't have to pay back. You can bootstrap it until you get some orders and cash coming in. You can start small, grow slow, and keep it simple.

6

Flip the Switch

MANUFACTURING IS so important because, at the end of the day, if you can't make your product at the right cost, you're not going to make a profit. Of course, a low production cost won't do you much good if your contract manufacturer doesn't consistently deliver quality products on time. To get the best bang for your buck, you need to find the right manufacturing partner and make sure you get what you're paying for. Remember, from your customers' point of view, you are the manufacturer.

That's why it's also important to provide the manufacturer with the information it needs to give you accurate price quotes and a product that meets your specifications. So before we get into how to find a good manufacturing partner, let's go over the things a contract manufacturer will need from you.

Product Design Package

Most contract manufacturers will ask for a *product design package,* the contents of which vary from industry to industry, manufacturer to manufacturer, and product to product. But they typically include a product specification, computer-aided design (CAD) drawings, and prototypes. Unless you have the ability and desire to create those components yourself, you'll need to hire out that work.

Some contract manufacturers can create prototypes for you, often at a reduced (or no) cost *if* you guarantee a purchase order of a certain amount. Some *manufacturing sourcing agents* (brokers who act as intermediaries between companies and contract manufacturers) also offer product development services.

Usually, you'll spend less and get your drawings and prototypes faster by hiring an industrial designer to do your CAD drawings and prototypes. Make sure that whoever creates your drawings and prototypes understands manufacturing and has expertise in your product category. You don't want to waste money and time designing something that can't actually be made. Be aware that the industrial designer you hire may bring on other professionals, such as an electrical engineer or a mechanical engineer.

To find an industrial designer or CAD engineer, you can reach out to the Industrial Design Society of America, use a website such as elance.com, or search the Internet. But a referral from someone you trust is best. Your contract manufacturer or sourcing agent may be able to refer someone to you. (On the flip side, your industrial designer may be able to refer you to some good contract manufacturers.) Ideally, you'll find someone local, which tends to make the process go smoother and faster.

Kick the tires before hiring anyone. Do some research and interview the person to make sure his or her qualifications match your needs. Ask for and check references. Ask to see samples of his or her work. Ask for a nondisclosure agreement (NDA); you may or may not get it. Another protection for you would be a work-for-hire agreement to avoid any coowner issues. Always get price quotes up front.

Product Specification

A *product specification* is basically a written description of your idea. The type of information needed depends on the product and manufacturer, and could include the following:

- Product type
- Product functions; what the product should do

- How long you expect the product to function; the life cycle of the product
- Product features; distinguishing characteristics
- Product dimensions or composition—for example, height, length, depth, thickness of walls, weight, viscosity
- Assembly or formulation instructions
- Any components to be used in the product—for example, a microchip or motor
- Any regulatory standards to which the product must comply
- Any performance metrics that must be met—for example, the amount of memory needed if the product is electronic

The more information you provide, the more accurate the manufacturer's price quote will be and the closer the sample production run will be to the product you want.

Technical Drawings

A contract manufacturer will need a visual rendering of your idea, even if it's just a sketch. Most will require a specific type of professionally created drawing—such as a CAD drawing, a three-dimensional mechanical drawing (such as a SolidWorks drawing), or a pattern (for sewn products).

GREAT (FREE) HELP IF YOU CAN GET IT
Leslie Haywood/Grill Charms

My contract manufacturer needed a 3D [three-dimensional] mechanical drawing called a SolidWorks. I didn't even know what that was! So I Googled it and found a local technical college that offered a program in SolidWorks and other CAD drawings. I called the instructor and asked if the class could help me. They created exactly what the manufacturer needed, and I didn't pay a cent for them!

I did the same thing with my packaging. I searched the Internet for a packaging designer and discovered that Clemson University in South Carolina has one of the best packaging science departments in the country. Who knew? I called the director and ended up being chosen as the senior project for their capstone class that year. Class members designed my packaging from start to finish. Not only did they make it aesthetically pleasing, they also did compression tests, vibration tests, and drop tests to make sure it could withstand the rigors of a 28-day ocean voyage from Taiwan, a cross-country train or truck ride from the port in Los Angeles, and double stacking of the pallets. And they did it all for free!

I received tens of thousands of dollars worth of professional work that I could never have afforded on my own—and I'm not alone. A lot of universities and colleges with specialized degree programs take on projects like mine. You just have to find out who's in charge, pick up the phone, and ask for what you need.

Prototypes

A *prototype* is a physical replica of your idea that represents what your product will look like and/or work like when it is manufactured. Prototypes teach you a lot about your idea. They can help you find ways to improve your design and produce your product in a more cost-effective manner.

You may have already built a mock-up, model, or a makeshift prototype of your product. For simple ideas, like a plush design, that type of *presentation prototype* may be sufficient for getting a price quote from a manufacturer, but you will still need to have a full-scale *preproduction prototype* that both looks like and works like the product you will be selling. For that, you'll need to hire a professional, who could be the contract manufacturer itself.

Annette Giacomazzi, inventor and founder of CastCoverZ, created her first prototypes by sewing them herself with material and elastic she bought at a local fabric store. She also made the initial patterns by hand. Then, she hired a professional patternmaker to create the computer-generated pattern the manufacturer required. The manufacturer in San Diego, California, that does her bulk manufacturing (she also has two local independent contractors for custom orders) made the preproduction prototypes.

Amy Baxter, inventor/founder of Buzzy, built a makeshift looks-like/works-like prototype with the casing of a cell phone to which she taped a vibrating "coin motor" using yellow-and-black electrical tape, applied in stripes to mimic a bee's body, as well as a pair of cold-pack "wings." After she'd made several prototypes to figure out the best placement for the motor and wings, she hired a local design firm to do the CAD drawings and full-scale prototypes. Similarly, David Mayer, inventor and founder of Clean Bottle, had 3D models and CAD renderings of his product made by local design professionals in Silicon Valley, but had his first working prototypes built by his contract manufacturer in China.

Whoever makes your prototypes should do the following:

- Sign a nondisclosure agreement and work-for-hire agreement
- Specialize in the specific type of prototype you need
- Build the prototype using materials, components, technologies, and processes that can be replicated in the factory if the product is mass-produced
- Build the prototype so it matches the actual size of the product as much as possible
- Build a prototype that looks good and works properly. It's one thing to have a pretty prototype; it's essential to have a functioning one
- Build more than one, because prototypes tend to break easily and you'll need them for multiple purposes

Packaging

Once you decide to move forward with a contract manufacturer, you'll need to provide your packaging specifications and artwork. I suggest getting your packaging together before you start looking for a manufacturer. At the very least, decide what verbiage and images you want on your packaging, and do some research and give some thought to the type of packaging you'll need and want. The contract manufacturer should be able to give you guidance on packaging, too.

In the beginning, it's wise to keep your packaging simple but professional. Many beginning entrepreneurs prioritize having special packaging custom-made, often overseas. But to get a good price, you usually have to order a large volume. You'll probably make numerous changes to your packaging design early on in the game. So I would be very cautious about spending a lot of money on fancy packaging you may have to dump.

Your packaging is an integral part of marketing your product, so its design and content should be consistent with the "image" and message you want your brand to convey. I suggest hiring a graphic artist with experience in packaging design.

I also recommend using a local printer and printing in small batches. The pricing may not be great, but it gives you more flexibility to test your packaging and to make design changes. You'll also get your packaging more quickly than with an overseas printer. To really save money, you may be able to print your packaging yourself using a high-quality laser printer.

At Hot Picks, we started off with standard, off-the-shelf packaging, did as much of the printing ourselves as we could, and ran small batches. Later, after we'd tested the market and knew what was working, we switched to custom packaging and ordered larger quantities.

We also packaged the guitar picks ourselves. It was kind of a pain to do, to be honest. It would have been better to have had the manufacturer pack the picks into the packages, but we were working with an American manufacturer and thought we could save money and increase our product markup by doing it ourselves. If you work with a foreign manufacturer, it will most likely do your packaging.

When you place your first purchase order with your contract manufacturer, you will need to create a *manufacturing and printing specification* (MAPS). This document specifies important information about your packaging, such as the quantity to be printed, the Pantones (standard colors used by printers worldwide), the type of card stock, trim size, where the hole for a peg will be, a list of artwork, how many units will be in the individual and master cartons, and any packing and delivery requirements. Along with the MAPS, you will need to provide the packaging artwork, usually a digital graphic file [in various formats such as EPS (Encapsulated PostScript) or JPEG (Joint Photographic Experts Group)] and a printed copy of the artwork.

PACKAGING: LESS IS MORE
David Mayer/Clean Bottle

When people are going down the aisle of a store, they're looking very quickly. So your packaging needs to grab their attention. For me, I've found that less is more. When your packaging has a clean look and some white space, it stands out. Then, take your product's most important benefit and hammer it. For example, our hang tag says only, "No more moldy bottles." We use that tag line on our tents and posters at trade shows, too. It's really provocative and has been super-effective. It stops people walking by and makes them wonder, *How do you get the mold out?* So they turn over the tag and read the product details on the back.

Labels

Certain products—such as toys, clothing, cosmetics, bedding, and pharmaceuticals—require certain information on their labels. Labeling laws and rules are established by various national and state/provincial regulatory bodies, such as the Food and Drug Administration (FDA) or Environmental Protection Agency (EPA). Ask your contract manufacturer about any special labeling requirements for your product. Since your contract manufacturer is a specialist in your product category, the questions you have should be answered with ease. You can also check with a trade association or an attorney who specializes in label law.

Industry Classification Number

Every type of business in the United States, Canada, and Mexico that produces, distributes, or sells products or services has a North

American Industry Classification System (NAICS) number. This six-digit numerical code represents the industry, industry sector, industry subsector, and industry group into which the company fits as well as its country of origin; for example, the NAICS for stuffed toy manufacturers in the United States is 339931. It is good to know what your NAICS is. Some federal and state agencies require businesses to have a NAICS code for government reporting and regulation purposes.

Bar Codes

A bar code is a small square with black-and-white vertical bars above a series of numbers that you see on almost every product you buy. The string of numbers is the Global Trade Item Number (GTIN) assigned to that specific product. More commonly known as a UPC (Universal Product Code) or EAN (European Article Number), a GTIN is a numerical code that identifies the company selling the item and that company's unique identification number for that item.

All major retailers, some independent retailers, and many e-commerce merchants require a UPC bar code for each item they sell. If you start out with only independent retailers selling your product, you may not need bar codes because many of those stores don't use bar codes. When you start branching out to larger and chain stores, or if you have a distributor, then you'll need a bar code for each of your products.

If you have only a handful of products, you might be able to use your manufacturer's bar code for your products. I know several small companies that do that, and it saves them the headache and expense of getting their own.

The nonprofit organization GS1 US (http://www.gs1us.org) authorizes and maintains all UPC/EAN codes. To get your own bar codes, you must become a member of GS1 US. This involves submitting an application (which you can do online) and paying a membership fee. The initial fee is based on your sales revenue and the number of UPCs you need, and currently runs as low as $760 for 100 UPCs. The membership renewal fee is currently $150 a year.

SKUs

SKU is the acronym for *stock-keeping unit*—the product identification code, often alphanumeric, used by retailers, distributors, and other merchants. Each merchant has its own SKU (pronounced "skyew") coding system, so each of your merchants may have a different SKU for each of your products. Often, but not always, the merchant will incorporate the manufacturer's UPC item reference number into its SKU. When retailers or distributors place an order with you and ask for your SKU, just give them your UPC item reference number for that product.

Finding the Right Manufacturer

The best advice I can give for finding a manufacturer is to shop around and use due diligence to qualify potential manufacturers. If you can get a referral from someone who has a product similar to yours, that's great. It's a good place to start. But never just take someone else's word for it, and never limit your search to just one or two companies. Find at least three contract manufacturers that specialize in your product category, and check each of them out thoroughly. Most contract manufacturers specialize in a given area, even if they make a lot of different products. If they specialize in products like yours, they are more likely to have the expertise to give you the price and product you want. If your product area is a small part of their business or new to them, it doesn't necessarily rule them out, but make sure they have the proven ability to do the job.

You should vigorously investigate any manufacturers you're considering. Visit their websites. Read their promotional literature. Check out their exhibits at trade shows. Do a web search for their names, and read whatever information comes up. Learn everything you can about what the manufacturers do, how they do it, and how well they do it.

Once you have identified a few contenders, contact them directly and ask for whatever other information you need. Find out which products they currently have on the line. Ask for customer references, and talk with those companies, if you can. Tour the manufacturers' facilities, and meet with their people. Make sure you understand their strengths and weaknesses. Some contract manufacturers will tell you they use certain technology when, in fact, they contract out that work and manage the process. You don't need another company to work with. Find a manufacturer that actually does the work.

If you decide to hire a manufacturing sourcing agent to help you line up a manufacturer, use the same due diligence to find the right one. Then, check out the manufacturer(s) they recommend.

Take the time to do your homework and find at least three manufacturers that meet your basic criteria. Then send each a request for quotation (RFQ) and see which one comes back with the combination of price, capabilities, and service you're looking for.

We'll talk about the RFQ process shortly. First, let's look at the pros and cons of contracting with a U.S. manufacturer versus an offshore manufacturer, and find out how to find both types.

Made in America

If you're located in the United States, I recommend starting off with a contract manufacturer that is also located in the United States if possible. Sometimes a product cannot be made in America because there is no factory with the capability to make it. Other times, it's just not affordable.

Affordability is the main reason so many companies go to low-cost countries (LCCs) where labor is cheap to manufacture their goods. China, India, Mexico, and Vietnam are but a few places companies choose. Manufacturing in the United States probably will cost you more, but if you can find a U.S. manufacturer that will produce your product at a price that allows a reasonable profit margin, I think it's worth it.

During the preproduction and early production stages, you will be going back and forth with the manufacturer to get your product right. You'll need to work closely and stay in constant communication. There is a lot of value in being able to converse in the same language during normal business hours with someone who is accustomed to the same culture and business methods. It is also valuable to be able to hop in your car or on a plane and actually go meet with someone as often as you want or need to. You can get up to speed faster and easier, better manage the process, more quickly resolve problems, and gain a better understanding of what goes into making your product. Ultimately, the result is a product that works well and meets your specifications.

Later, after you've worked out the bugs and streamlined the process, it might make sense to order large quantities from abroad.

Some companies are doing the exact opposite: they are using an offshore contract manufacturer to keep costs down during the early stages of their business and bringing manufacturing to the United States once they are turning a profit. In fact, three of the startups featured in this book—Buzzy, Clean Bottle, and CelebriDucks—started out manufacturing in China but have since moved some or all of their manufacturing to the States. Yes, it's most likely cost them more by doing so, and they've probably made less money. At the end of the day, they've had the control, quality, ease of doing business, and peace of

BRINGING IT HOME
Craig Wolfe/CelebriDucks

I spent the last year talking to factories and printers, gearing up to move our manufacturing from China to America. We will be the only company making rubber ducks in the United States, where they were invented, in the state of Ohio, where it all began. I'm proud of that, but it also makes me sad because there are no other factories and not enough trained mold makers and painters to make them here.

Even the gift box I put my ducks in will be printed in the United States. It's 10 times the cost to print them in the short runs like I do, but I'm not importing boxes from overseas! Whatever the cost, I'll absorb it. I'll make less. If I had shareholders, I'd be fired! But I will make them here, and I will sell more. Because I believe that in the long run, enough people will care that we took an industry that was invented here and brought it back.

mind they wanted, which are the same reasons Annette Giacomazzi of CastCoverZ went with a U.S. contract manufacturer to begin with.

At Hot Picks, we were able to go with a local manufacturer right at the start because the machine used to rapidly print guitar picks requires little labor to operate, making the cost of manufacturing in the United States doable. We hired Dunlop to make most of our picks and another local company, Extreme Graphics, for some of our designs. I loved being able to call people there during normal business hours and speak in English, since that is the language I am fluent in. We built a great relationship. It was simple, and we got our product fast.

Another advantage of manufacturing in the United States is that it is usually easier and faster to make changes to products and add new products. To stay competitive and grow your business, you have to come up with something fresh every few months. For example, at Hot Picks we knew that a few vampire movies were coming out. Because we were small and nimble, quickly designing a vampire guitar pick was a no-brainer. Because our manufacturer was in the States, we were able to get them produced and in stores in time to take advantage of that opportunity. That's difficult to do with most overseas manufacturers.

Here are some ways to find good American manufacturers:

- Ask someone who has a product similar to yours for the name of his or her company's contract manufacturer.
- Ask for referrals from a local or online inventors' or small business group.
- Search online manufacturing directories, such as Thomas Registry of American Manufacturers (http://www.thomasnet .com), MacRAE's Blue Book (http://www.macraesbluebook.com), and MFG.com (http://www.mfg.com).
- Do a web search for "contract manufacturer" and for your product type (e.g., "contract manufacturer ladders").
- Search social media networks such as LinkedIn (http://www .linkedin.com).
- Call the trade associations in your field and ask for recommendations.

- Attend a trade show where contract manufacturers in your industry are exhibitors.
- Check the classified advertisements in the back of a trade magazine catering to your industry.

SOURCING AGENTS: YOUR BEST WEAPON IN THE WILD, WILD EAST
Rob Stephani/Hot Picks USA

We made most of our guitar picks in the United States and about 5 percent overseas. We were lucky in that a guy I grew up with has a manufacturing sourcing business with offices in China, Malaysia, and Taiwan, and they set up everything. I wouldn't do it any other way, because it's like the Wild, Wild East over there. Things change quickly. Things go wrong. So you really need to have a sourcing agent you trust. You also need to go over there to meet the manufacturer and see what's going on in the factory. You should definitely check your prototypes, preproduction runs, and the first few small orders to make sure everything is right as rain before you start ordering huge quantities and spending big dollars.

Offshore Manufacturing

I got my first taste of manufacturing overseas when I was hired as employee number 20 at Worlds of Wonder (WOW). I hadn't been there long when my boss, Dave Small, sent me overseas to monitor production at our factories in China, Thailand, and Taiwan. He said I'd be there a couple of weeks; it ended up being months. It was definitely a learning experience. One of the things I learned is that, even when you're standing next to the production line, things can go sideways. When that happened while I was at the factory, I was able to work with the people there to get back on track. But when I left, problems and confusion arose, and I was no longer there to resolve the issues.

You really have to stay on top of it. Paying for one-half or one-third of your order up front is standard but not being able to check it first is nerve-racking! Even when the initial samples and the first couple of production runs look good, quality can drop over time.

I think your best bet is to work with a manufacturing sourcing agent. This is a service you'll have to pay for, but having an intermediary on the ground working on your behalf—someone who knows the language and the culture and has experience working with manufacturers, suppliers, and freight forwarders in a particular country and your industry—will save you a lot of headaches and maybe even some money in the long run.

If I were having my product manufactured overseas, I wouldn't even consider doing it myself. I'd team up with a good one-stop shop like Global Sourcing Specialists (http://www.productgss.com). It is priceless to be connected with a company that knows who's good and who's not in a given country or region, and who has the connections to get you the lowest price and the highest value. WOW used sourcing agents when I was there, and they were very helpful.

Even when you use a good sourcing agent, though, things can get dicey, especially if the manufacturer has to change its tooling or processes. It took Clean Bottle three years, four different factories, and a lot of trial and error to get its production running smoothly in China.

Clean Bottle's president, David Mayer, explains: "Most factories in China are good at copying but not so good at doing something unique. I had to show them testimonials from people to convince them there was a big market for my bottles and that purchase orders for fifty thousand units would come pretty soon if they'd help us out with these five thousand."

The best way to find an offshore manufacturer on your own is to get referrals from people who have products similar to yours being made overseas. Another way is to check with the trade council for that country or region. These trade associations, which are similar to the American Chamber of Commerce, can be found on the Internet. You can also search an online directory of manufacturers, such as Alibaba (http://www.alibaba.com), which is huge and has manufacturers all over the world. You can also do an Internet search for offshore contract manufacturers in your product category. Do your homework to make sure they are on the up and up. Be alert to scams. Use good judgment. To minimize the risk, use a sourcing agent.

NEAR AND FAR: DESIGN TO PRODUCTION
Nancy Tedeschi/SnapIt

I hired a mechanical design engineer to do a CAD drawing. For my prototype, I Googled "optical screw manufacturers" and found one located four hours from my home. I went to his facility and showed him the drawing. Less than three weeks later, my prototypes—a run of ten thousand screws—were ready. The screws worked right off the bat! That guy knew what he was doing, which was really important, because if I hadn't found him or someone like him, I wouldn't have known what to do. Unfortunately, he couldn't manufacture them at my price point. So I ended up going overseas, which happened in a sort of backward fashion.

I managed to get a little blurb with a photo of my screw in the "What's New?" column of a trade magazine. About a week after the magazine came out, I got a call from an optometrist who asked for some samples. He loved them so much he got me an appointment with the distributor he bought his supplies from. I gave the distributor an exclusive agreement for U.S. distribution, and they gave me $100,000 up front. The distributor then referred me to a contract manufacturer in China. I still have that manufacturer as well as a second manufacturer in China that I found on Alibaba.com. I also have a contact in China who does quality control checks for me.

Getting a Quote

For all the manufacturers you are considering using, you need to know what they are going to do, how long it's going to take, and what it's going to cost. The usual method of obtaining that information is with a *request for quotation* (RFQ). This document, which you will put together, standardizes the information you receive from different manufacturers. The benefit of creating an RFQ is when you review the bids, you're comparing like things instead of trying to translate what each bid is either offering or not offering. When you create your RFQ, you set the parameters of what needs to be addressed by a potential manufacturer. This will better enable you to choose the right company to manufacture your product.

Your RFQ might request a price quote and estimated timeline to complete certain preproduction "deliverables" (or "milestones"), such as:

- Prototype
- Preproduction pilot (also called a "desktop engineering pilot")—a small production run to iron out any product design, manufacturing engineering, and tooling bugs
- First article test, inspection, and approval
- Production pilot—a final, small production run to prove the tooling, machining, production line, and assembly processes

Your RFQ should ask for production costs by quantity breaks—for example, the price for orders of 5,000 units, 20,000 units, and 50,000 units. It might also ask for a breakdown of labor, materials, and packaging/labeling costs.

Your RFQ might also ask for the following information:

Tooling. Is any special tooling needed to manufacture your product? If so, at what cost, if any, to you? Some contract manufacturers will absorb this cost; others will pass it on to you.

Minimum order. Does the manufacturer have a minimum order requirement? If so, what is it (in units or a dollar amount)?

Lead time. How many days or weeks after the manufacturer receives your purchase order will it ship your product? Do any variables affect lead times—for example, the size of the order or the time of the year?

Materials options. You will be taxed based on the materials that make up your product. Ask the manufacturer to suggest materials that will help lower costs without sacrificing quality. You can find a materials tariff schedule at the U.S. International Trade Commission's website (http://www.usitc.gov).

Packaging options. Can the manufacturer recommend a more effective or cheaper way to package your product?

Certifications. How is the manufacturer qualified to do what it does? Is the company certified by Walmart, Target, and/or Disney? Is it "ISO certified"—signifying that its quality-management systems adhere to the standards established by the International Organization for Standardization (ISO)?

Customers. Who does the company make products for? Ask for references.

Product storage options. Can the manufacturer store product for you if you place a large order? The manufacturer might charge you a small storage fee, but the volume discount on the larger production run will likely reduce your production costs.

Packing options. Will the manufacturer pack the products for shipment and storage? If so, how and what are the costs?

Payment terms. Does the manufacturer require a portion of the payment up front? When are additional payments due? How will you pay—in U.S. dollars, by check, by electronic bank transfer? Does the manufacturer need a letter of credit from your bank?

Defective products. Ask about the manufacturer's policies regarding defective products. Make sure you get the information in writing. All of the manufacturers I've worked with have been accommodating about fixing mistakes. Even when they make it right and at no additional cost to you (which is what you want), you may run into a timing issue if your retailers need product before the manufacturer can replace the defective run. A good way to prevent that from happening is to always keep a little inventory on hand, so you still have product to offer if a shipment comes in with defects.

Before submitting RFQs to contract manufacturers, have them sign a nondisclosure agreement that includes a noncompete clause. Submit your product design package along with your RFQ.

When you receive all the RFQs back from the manufacturers, review and compare them carefully. If you have any questions or need additional information, contact the manufacturer (or the sourcing agent). Never automatically go with the cheapest pricing. Always go for the best value and the best fit for you. You might also want to give your second choice a small order now and then, so you have a backup if you get a large order that your main manufacturer can't handle alone or if things suddenly go wrong with your main manufacturer.

Logistics

Before you place your first purchase order with your contract manufacturer, you should figure out how you're going to transport your product from the manufacturer's factory to your warehouse (which initially might be your home) as well as to your distributor(s) and customers.

If you're based in the United States or Canada and you're manufacturing and selling product only in North America, you can probably manage your own freight. For smaller shipments, you might use the U.S. Postal Service (USPS), United Parcel Service (UPS), and/or FedEx. For larger shipments, you might use one or more trucking companies, perhaps a regional carrier and an interstate carrier like Hunt Transportation or Con-way.

The more links there are in your supply chain, the more complicated it becomes to manage your freight and shipping costs. If you find yourself in this situation, it probably makes sense to hire a freight forwarder to handle all or a portion of your shipments.

If you're manufacturing and/or selling product overseas, I definitely think you should use a freight forwarder. Freight forwarders can set up and manage all your shipments—whether you're transporting goods overseas, across the continent (for example, Mexico or Canada), or cross-country, by ship, air, rail, or truck. They will help you with customs, tariffs, and so on. They will also find the best way to get your shipments delivered on time and at the lowest possible cost.

At Hot Picks, we had accounts all over the world and used a lot of freight forwarders. They were wonderful, completing all our paperwork and picking up right from our office. A couple of times, customers received an order with items listed on the packing slip but missing from the order, and we could never figure out what caused the shortages. When materials go missing in transit like that, it's called *leakage*.

You can save money by having your shipments put in the same shipping container (ocean, air, rail, or truck) with another company's shipments. It's called *less-than-container* (LTC) shipping. Sometimes, we had our manufacturer in China ship directly to a distributor, which was convenient and saved in freight costs. Another way to save money is to *consolidate* your freight—combining several *inbound* shipments from the same area (say, your two factories in Hong Kong) or several *outbound* shipments to the same area (say, a distributor and four major customers on the East Coast) in the same shipping container. Talk to your freight forwarder or carrier about these two options.

Getting Off to a Good Start

Knowing who is going to manufacture your product and how you're going to transport it *before* you start getting orders from customers will go a long way in getting you off to a good start. Once you start producing and selling your product, you'll need to manage your inventory and your vendors to stay on track.

Keep a Tight Rein on Inventory

You should buy an initial amount of inventory so that you always have some in stock. If a retailer orders your product, you need to be able to get it to them on time. It sends a bad message if you can't or don't. When they want it, they want it now. They're dedicating shelf space to your product, and if they can't fill that space with your product now, they'll put something else there. If your contract manufacturer has a minimum order requirement, that might be enough product to keep on hand early in the game.

Don't get obsessed with ordering big quantities at first. Getting a volume price break is beneficial, but not if it means you have a stockpile of product it takes you months to sell.

You don't want to have too much or too little product on hand, so you need to think ahead. You also don't want any surprises, so you need to be able to "see" what's on hand, what's coming in, and what's going out.

When you start out small, storing and managing inventory is relatively simple. Hopefully, you can use your office or garage as your "warehouse" in the beginning.

You can begin organizing your inventory by considering some metrics: How long does it take to receive product from your manufacturer—from the day you submit the purchase order until the day it arrives at your door? How long do you have to fill customer orders? This will help with the planning aspect of managing your inventory.

At some point, you might need or want to invest in a computerized inventory management system. There are many off-the-shelf inventory management software programs for small to midsized businesses, including some that work with accounting programs such as QuickBooks. They range in price from approximately $1,000 to more than $20,000. In the beginning, you can probably keep track of your inventory visually, by organizing the product in your warehouse and eyeballing it constantly, and by creating an Excel spreadsheet or a chart on which you record everything coming in, going out, and on hand.

At Hot Picks, we kept track of our inventory in a few ways. We stored it so we could quickly and easily see how much of each SKU was on hand. We also matched the inventory going in and out with our books. I found a company in town that was selling a lot of product and looked at how it managed inventory. I found the same things were being done within that company that we were doing in ours.

Get Close to Your Vendors

It's critical to understand and keep close tabs on every link in your supply chain—your manufacturer, sourcing agent, freight forwarder, warehouse, or whatever. Meet the people who make your business work, and build a good relationship with each of these key vendors.

I encourage you to visit your contract manufacturer at the very beginning, if you can, and then on a routine basis or when a problem arises. I always visit the facilities that make my product and get to know the general manager. It is also extremely important to build relationships with the people on the line. I try to understand any problems they are having, and I ask questions. "Is there any way to make the product better?" "What can we do to reduce the cost?" "Is there anything I can do to help you produce a better product?" It's one thing to take a tour and talk to management about orders, but making a connection with the people on the line who are doing the actual work every day is invaluable. Without them, you don't have a business.

This is yet another benefit to having a small business: you can meet all these people, and they can get to know you. If you have the time, take some of them out to lunch, dinner, or drinks. Do whatever you can to build a strong relationship. Then, if you have any problems, it's easier to call them up and talk about it.

Keep abreast of new technologies, too. I've seen the manufacturing of my product change over the years. If you understand the process and stay close to your manufacturer, you can work together to reduce costs, improve efficiencies, and prevent and solve problems.

• • •

Finding the right contract manufacturer and setting up your supply chain *before* you start selling, producing, and shipping product are critical to successfully bringing your idea to market yourself. Of course, you're always going to have to keep on top of your inventory and your vendors, especially your contract manufacturer(s). That's a lot easier to do when you start out small and stay close to the process from the moment you flip on the switch and throughout the life of your business.

7

Power Marketing Made Simple

O F ALL the hats a new inventor-entrepreneur has to wear, marketing is often one of the most ill-fitting . . . and always among the most important. With consumers bombarded by so much information about so many products, how do you get them to notice yours? With big companies spending big bucks on massive, multilevel marketing campaigns, how do you ensure that stores want to sell your product and consumers want to buy it?

I have no formal training or background in marketing, and I used to feel insecure about that. Living with a corporate marketing executive with an MBA (my wife, Janice) has been a little intimidating, too. But I've always recognized the importance of marketing. It's everything, in my opinion. In fact, marketing is, or should be, a consideration in every aspect of your business, because it all impacts how the marketplace views you. That's why it's so important to understand marketing and use it wisely.

Basically, marketing is taking deliberate actions to make your target audience want to buy your product. If you build it, they will not just come. First, you must produce a unique product in a desirable package and at the right price, and then you have to promote it.

In fact, if you've studied and tested the market and determined who your competitors and potential customers are and what your competitive edge is, you've already taken the first steps in the marketing process. Armed with that information, you can now move on to the next steps: creating your brand and marketing your product.

What's Brand Got to Do with It?

Your *brand* is how your target audience perceives you. *Branding* is defining how you want to be perceived and then cultivating that perception in the marketplace by conveying a certain image and making a promise to your target audience. A brand is actually built over time, and it is based not only on the image and promise you put out there but also on how well you live up to them.

Branding is an integral part of marketing that also extends to every facet of your business, especially to product design, sales, and customer service. Building a strong brand has a whole lot to do with the successful marketing of your product and, ultimately, the success of your business.

Defining Your Brand Image and Promise

The first step in building your brand is deciding the image and promise you want to communicate. That process begins with you asking yourself a few simple questions: "What is my product about? What makes it different? Who is my target audience? What makes them tick? What do they want that my product is uniquely able to give? What feelings do I want to evoke in the target audience? What traits and qualities do I want them to associate with my brand? What's my product's "special sauce"—the thing that sets it apart and will attract customers to my brand?"

To answer those questions for whatever brand I'm working on, I study the market. I investigate my competition. I look at competitors' products, packaging, brand names, logos, and tag lines. I check out their websites, advertising, brochures, media coverage, promotions, and so on. I make note of the key points they are making and how those are being expressed. I determine what their niches are, who their customers are, and what attracts those customers to those brands. I identify their brand images and promises, and I try to understand why they created the brands the way they did.

Then, I investigate my target audience—the niche that's the best match for my product. What do they look like, talk like, act like? What do they enjoy, need, and want? What are their demographics, interests, values, lifestyles? What culture or subculture do they fit into? What other products do they buy?

At the end of the day, I want to create a brand image that stands out in the marketplace and appeals to my target audience. At Hot Picks, we wanted to be cool, current, and a little edgy. In the beginning, our niche was the heavy metal crowd. We had a good time creating our brand, and consumers responded positively.

Decide on your niche, and tailor your brand to it. Don't try to appeal to everyone. You can always add to your brand image later, after you have some recognition in the marketplace and are ready to expand your product line. As an example, after Hot Picks was established with the heavy metal crowd, we designed a new line of picks called Girls Rock. To introduce this line extension, we used our same brand logo but changed the colors and other graphic design elements on the package.

Using language, visual elements, and cultural references, you can create whatever look, feel, mood, attitude, and personality you want. The design might be peaceful, hard-edged, corporate, industrial, down-home, high-tech, traditional, cutting-edge, artsy, sporty, youthful, mature, fun, sophisticated, luxurious, adventurous, preppy, urban, global, "green," or whatever; the list can go on and on. Just make sure the design fits you and your target audience. Use your creativity to come up with an image and promise that are unique in the marketplace, relevant to your target audience, and authentic to you.

Creating Your Brand Identity

Building brand recognition in the marketplace begins with creating a strong *brand identity*. Your brand identity, or *business identity,* is your company name, logo, and tag line along with any visual elements (e.g., color scheme, graphics, symbols, shapes, and caricatures) or audio elements (e.g., jingles and sound effects) you want associated with your brand. It also includes the name of your product (or product lines) as well as the look and feel of your packaging.

Whatever elements you include in your brand identity, make sure they fit your product and your target audience and work well together. If your product is animal-shaped, organic-cotton pillows for children, you don't want a slick, high-tech brand identity, nor do you want one element of your identity to contradict another. For example, if your company name is Good Earth Toys and your tag line is "Safe, eco-friendly fun for kids," you wouldn't want your logo to be a jet-black rectangle with your name and tag line printed in silver. People typically associate green and blue colors, not black and silver, with something that is eco-friendly. The visuals that accompany your product will have an impact on your customers, so step back and think about what will best represent your product line and make people want to purchase your product over another.

Your brand identity should also have some staying power. As a rule of thumb, you'll want your company name, logo, and tag line to be relevant for at least five years and preferably ten. It's fine to tweak your brand identity a little bit; in fact, it may be necessary in order to keep up with market trends and your company's growth. But *rebranding*—switching to a whole new image—tends to be a difficult, costly, and risky undertaking. It's smarter to start off with the right brand identity and stick with it for a while.

I suggest coming up with at least three different options for each of your main brand elements—your company name, tag line, and logo—and running them by your family, friends, mentor, colleagues, and potential customers. Ask them what they like and dislike about each trademark you're considering. Ask what image and emotion it evokes. Ask which trademark they like best.

Once you come up with a name, tag line, or logo you like, always conduct a trademark search to make sure no one else is using it or something very similar to it. After you've nailed down an original trademark for your business, register it with the U.S. Patent and Trademark Office.

Choose a Strong Brand Name and Tag Line

Your company name and product name(s) are both *brand names*. Sometimes the company name and product name are the same, but often they are different. A *tag line* (*slogan* or *brand tag*) is a catchy phrase that reflects the promise you're making to customers.

A brand name can be descriptive, like iPad and Ziploc, or alliterative, like Jelly Belly and Roto-Rooter, or evocative, like Little Einsteins and Wrangler. It can be or include the founder's name(s), like Ben & Jerry's Ice Cream and Harley-Davidson. A brand name can be a fictional character, like Mr. Clean and Mrs. Butterworth's. It can be a made-up word (that is, a *neologism*), like Google (derived from the mathematical term "googol") and Calgon (calcium + gone). It can even be an acronym, like BMW (Bavarian Motor Works) and IBM (International Business Machines).

My priorities in finding a name were that it could be trademarked and would evoke the image we were going for. We chose Hot Picks because the name had attitude and we had a hot new product! What initially sparked the name, though, was that our first products featured images of "hot chicks" on the picks. Even though that product line was short-lived, we kept the name because it still applied.

At first, our tag line was "The coolest guitar picks on the planet." Later, it became "The largest selection of picks," and now it's "Home of the original skull shaped picks!" The tag line for my Spinformation label is "75% more space, just by turning the label."

John Ferrell, my patent attorney and an expert on branding and trademarks, says a strong brand name or tag line is both suggestive and percussive; it implies what your business or product is about and has an engaging rhythm when you hear or speak it. A percussive word or phrase patterns itself in the brain, which makes it memorable. Being memorable is great!

Here are a few famous brand names and tag lines that fit John's definition to a tee:

Ajax: Stronger than dirt.
Energizer: Keeps going and going and going.
PlayStation: Live in your world, play in ours.
Timex: It takes a licking and keeps on ticking.

Some people suggest choosing a business name that begins with one of the first five or six letters of the alphabet so that it appears in the beginning of an alphabetized directory. Today, with most people searching for things on the Internet, I think it is important for your brand name to be the same as your domain (website) name.

TIP

THE POWER OF A DOMAIN

Your domain name (URL, or "uniform resource locator") is the "address" of your website. Ideally, your domain name should be the same as your brand name. That's why it's important to choose your brand and domain names at the same time and to reserve your URL immediately, even if you don't have a website yet. Search the Internet for domain names similar to the brand name you're considering. If someone has already reserved that domain name, I suggest choosing a different brand name for which the domain is available.

I also suggest reserving both the *.com* and *.net* extensions of your domain. If they are not available, don't settle for any of the other available extensions, like *.biz* or *.us*. In people's minds and for search engine rankings, *.com* and *.net* are the top dogs.

Design a Distinctive Logo

A *logo* is a visual mark that instantly identifies your brand. There are three types of logos:

- A *wordmark*; the brand name in stylized text, such as the Google logo

- A symbol, emblem, icon, or other graphic, such as Target's bull's-eye or the Nike swoosh
- A wordmark and graphics, such as "McDonald's" and the two golden arches

Many logos have a specific color scheme, too. The Facebook logo, for example, is the word "facebook" (lowercase) in white type against a blue background.

An effective logo is eye-catching, original, and memorable. If you want to check out the logos of some of the most successful brands of all time, visit the Famous Logos website (http://www.famouslogos.us).

I think having your logo designed by a graphic designer is money well spent. If you shop around, you should be able to find a good graphic designer willing to design a logo for $300 to $1,000.

Here are a few ways to find graphic/logo designers:

- Get a referral from a company whose logo you like.
- Contact the graphic design instructor at your local college or university and ask for a referral of a talented student or recent graduate.
- Post a "logo design contest" on a crowd-sourcing site, such as 99 Designs (http://www.99designs.com), DesignCrowd (http://www .designcrowd.com), and Logo Design Guru (http://www.logo designguru.com).
- Use a freelance job sourcing site, such as Mediabistro (http:// www.mediabistro.com), Elance (http://www.elance.com), and Guru (http://www.guru.com).

When you're working with a designer, don't just give him or her your brand name, tag line, and the colors you like. Give the designer as much information as possible about your target audience, your product, and the image and message you want your brand to convey.

Always check out the designer's portfolio to make sure the person you are interested in hiring has experience designing logos and you like his or her work. Get a price quote upfront. Ask whether the designer uses *royalty-free clip art*. If so, you won't be able to trademark your logo because other people can use the same clip art in their logos.

Stand Out with Brand-Building Packaging

Your product packaging makes a big impression on consumers. It also affects how retailers market and sell your product in their stores. So consider what your packaging design will communicate to your target audience. Does it have the right look and feel? Does it give them the information they need and express it in the right way? Will it stand out from other products on store shelves? Is it memorable?

Your packaging can and should encompass intellectual property elements, ranging from your brand name (trademark), logo, and tag line (trademark and service mark), and the shape and design of the package itself (legally protected by *trade dress,* a product's distinct physical appearance, including shape, size, and color; think about the shape of the Coca-Cola bottle). If your package has some functionality to it, as my Spinformation labels do, then you might be able to patent it.

Make sure, too, that your packaging doesn't encroach on anyone else's trademark. For example, at Hot Picks we began to market and sell our guitar picks in packages shaped like coffins. We ran ads in magazines to promote them, and lo and behold, the attorney for Coffin Case guitar cases contacted us immediately! We had to stop using that new package because our competitor's trademark was too strong.

Give Them a Wow Brand Experience!

What your brand image and promise say about you has a huge impact on your target market. That's why choosing the right brand name, tag line, and logo is so important. But I believe what you do to live up to that image and promise is more important and has more impact on your brand. At the end of the day, it is the *brand experience* you create for your customers that strengthens or weakens your brand. The best way to build a strong brand is to provide a great product and great customer service.

Be your brand's ambassador. Exemplify what your brand stands for in all of your business dealings—with customers, vendors, employees, the media, at industry meet-ups, and in the public eye. Make sure any partners and employees represent your brand appropriately, too. After all, the people who answer your phone are working the front line;

they may provide the first impression a potential customer has of your brand. Make sure they are friendly, remain professional, and present the right image.

Always provide incredible products and customer service so your customers want to talk about it. Whatever you do, leverage the power of your customers' voice! Post customer testimonials on your website and in your marketing literature. If a customer writes a great review of your product on a social media page, blog, magazine, Amazon.com, or wherever, provide a link to the review on your website. Always send a personal thank-you note or small gift to anyone who gives you a positive review or testimonial. Some people buy products solely based on reviews and testimonials. They are a great way to build trust and confidence. You can even ask your customers to write a review or give you a testimonial. Big companies fear reviews because they don't like the negative ones. One or two bad reviews are okay; you can't please everyone. Just don't let the good word people are spreading about your product go unnoticed.

Create Demand and Drive Sales

Your product is finished, your packaging looks great, and your trademarks are spot-on. Now, it's time to get word out and draw customers in. But you don't have much money to spend on marketing. Do you advertise in magazines, TV, radio, or online? Launch direct mail and telemarketing campaigns? Exhibit at trade shows? Blog, Tweet, eBlast, webcast, podcast? Create flyers, brochures, product sheets, signs, posters, store displays? Send out a flurry of press releases? Run special promotions? All of the above?

There is no one right answer. Only you can determine which marketing tactics to use, because it depends on your preferences, abilities, products, budget, customers, and industry. So instead of talking about all the marketing tactics available to you, I'm going to talk about a new approach to marketing and some simple, affordable, and effective ways to implement it.

Marketing in Today's Rapidly Changing World

The old-school approach to marketing focuses on using "push" marketing tactics, such as advertising and direct mail, that interrupt consumers—for example, while they're watching TV, listening to the radio, reading a magazine, surfing the Internet, or opening their mail—to promote a brand. Push marketing is all about getting your message in front of as many people as possible in the hope that some of them will become customers. Typically, 2 to 3 percent do—*if* you've sent out a lot of messages to a lot of people. And doing that eventually becomes very expensive.

In today's consumer-centric, wired world, where brand preference or rejection can be made, changed, and shared instantly, push marketing doesn't work so well. Frankly, I don't think it has ever worked well for startups and small businesses. As a new business, there simply isn't enough money to buy customers with expensive advertising and marketing tactics. It takes time to earn people's attention and business.

What I've realized is that you need to make your product and your customers' experience with your product about your customers, not about you. That means you have to understand your customers and focus your marketing efforts on communicating your willingness and ability to give them what they want and need. It's not about selling products; it's about building relationships and providing value.

Jim Horan, author of the bestselling book *One Page Business Plan* and founder/CEO of One Page Business Plan Company, once said to me, "Before you can eat from the village, you need to feed the village." That's what the new school of *pull marketing* is all about: instead of sending a flyer to everyone in the village asking them to buy your product, you reach out to the most influential people in the village and give them something of value—information, enjoyment, or assistance. You make a personal connection with them. You earn their trust. You give them products they want. And they tell everyone in their village how great you are! Then, the people in that village tell people in other villages. Before you know it, you've got people in villages far and wide seeking you out, buying your products, and encouraging their family, friends, and colleagues to do the same.

This is *word-of-mouth marketing* on steroids! With the Internet, especially social media networks, the "word"—good or bad—can spread like wildfire. If customers love you, they can sing your praises to the world. If they don't, they can give you a big thumbs-down that travels with the speed of light. So you'd better deliver great products and great customer service!

But it takes more than having a product people like and being nice to people who buy it to create an army of impassioned evangelists who turn other people on to you. In this brave new world of marketing, you have a new set of marching orders, namely:

Be remarkable. Seth Godin, bestselling author on the topic of marketing, had it right when he said, "You've got to be a purple cow." You can't just blend in with the herd. You have to stand out and give people something to talk about—something positive and extraordinary. Don't just be different; be outstanding.

Be personal. Even with all the technology wiring us all together, it's still the personal touch that matters. People still want to be "linked" with someone they know and like. They still want a "friend" who understands and helps them. Get to know your customers, and let them know you.

Be accessible. People want to have one-on-one interactions with real human beings. Companies that don't have two-way forms of customer communication are dinosaurs. Provide your customers with easy ways to communicate with you. Invite them to share their wants, needs, likes, dislikes, questions, and concerns. Respond quickly, and communicate directly whenever possible.

Be genuine. Customers want to know you're the real deal. Learn from others, but follow your gut and cut your own path. Don't try to be all things to all people, and don't pretend to be something you're not. Be yourself.

Be transparent. Nobody likes to be surprised or feel duped. Say what you do, and do what you say. When things go wrong, admit it. Consumers have access to so much information today that attempting to cover up something is a bad idea. People make mistakes. Be human. Be honest. Make it right.

Be relevant. Consumers want products tailored to their specific needs and wants. As their needs and wants change, they want the brands they're familiar with to change with them. Stay close to your customers, and innovate for the market.

I look at marketing as the process of building relationships. The question is: how do you do that without it costing you an arm and a leg? I feel the key is to find people and organizations that have a huge network of followers who might benefit from your product or expertise. Reach out to them and contribute what you can. Find a way to support them and their intentions, and they will support you.

Your Website: Not Just a Pretty Face

A website is so much more than a static online promotional piece for your products and company. It is also a powerful tool for attracting and interacting with customers. Websites that don't provide opportunities for interaction and dialogue don't really work anymore. This can be rather delicate at times, because once you've brought everyone together to talk about your product, it opens the door for criticism and complaints. Be sure to monitor customer comments, and respond quickly and professionally.

In terms of web design, a clean, attractive layout with short blocks of text and compelling graphics is always a good bet, but don't be afraid to be creative and have some fun with it. Just make sure the look, feel, and content are appropriate for your brand and target audience. Your site should have clearly labeled tabs and icons and an intuitive structure so that it is easy for visitors to navigate your site and find what they are looking for.

Your website should also include the following:

- Key words in the site description, page tags, and content headings—for search engine optimization (SEO)
- Forum and/or blog with comment capabilities so visitors can communicate with you and with one another

- Contact mechanisms—a contact form and/or e-mail link, as well as your phone number
- Products page (or online catalog)
- Store locator—the names, locations, and links of retailers that sell your products
- Links throughout content, so visitors can click to access additional content on your site and other sites
- Share functionality—plug-ins to your social media pages, such as Facebook, Pinterest, and Twitter, so visitors can share the content on your site
- Links to your social media pages
- Media page—for posting all your press releases, showcasing media coverage you've received, and including a link for providing/requesting your media kit and a link for the media to contact you
- Online store, with shopping cart and e-commerce payment capabilities (such as PayPal), if you plan to sell your product directly to consumers online
- Merchants page—for communicating with retailers and distributors; not accessible to consumers

At some point, you might also want to add webcast, podcast, and mobile web capabilities.

Social Media: Your New Best Friend

Social media is not advertising. You have to master the social part before you get to the media part. Don't start any social media marketing by immediately talking to others about your product. You need to be social, remember? Get to know others; ask them questions; eventually, lead them into conversations about your category or problems you encounter. Then, introduce your product. You don't want to scare off any potential friends by being overly aggressive. No one likes to be sold to on social media sites.

I love social media sites. They're great for getting to know your customers and letting them get to know you; soliciting feedback on new products and improvements; fielding customer questions and complaints; keeping customers up-to-date on what you're doing; offering special promotions; and so much more. Just make sure you're using it effectively. If you're just trying to sell, you're missing the boat. A good ratio is 80 percent sharing and 20 percent promoting/selling.

Share your story, and encourage your social media pals to share theirs. Share content and events your target audience will find interesting, inspiring, helpful, or enjoyable. Invite them to share their thoughts, feelings, and activities, and acknowledge them when they do. If they send you photos with your product, post them! Offer discounts and awards available only to your social media friends.

Posting short messages a few times a day is ideal. When you can't post in real time, create messages in advance and schedule their release. Don't let too many days go by without responding to comments and interacting in real time, and don't go overboard. Posting too much annoys people and takes up too much of your time.

You don't need to be on every social media network. Do some homework and choose the two or three favored by your target audience. The two most used sites at this time are Facebook (http://www .facebook.com) and Twitter (https://twitter.com), with Google+ (www .google.com/+) gaining favor. LinkedIn (http://www.linkedin.com) is popular for business-to-business networking, and Pinterest (http:// pinterest.com) is like a giant pinboard where people share products and other "things you love." YouTube is also becoming a great social media tool for inventor-entrepreneurs.

HOW WE ROCKED SOCIAL MEDIA BEFORE SOCIAL MEDIA WAS COOL

We launched Hot Picks in 2002, and by 2005, we were selling in a number of stores. But we wanted to grow, and I was looking for ways to increase consumer demand for our product. That's when I stumbled across MySpace (http://www.myspace.com). I discovered that thousands of garage bands were using MySpace to share their music and that their fans were extremely loyal. So, we set up an account and put photos of Hot Picks on our MySpace page. We asked bands to be our friends, then we asked their fans to be friends.

We were building a community on MySpace, but I felt we needed to give them more incentive to buy our products. That's when it hit me: we couldn't get big-name bands to endorse Hot Picks, but all these garage bands were dying for recognition. Why not give them our endorsement? So we set up a campaign on our website, Hot Picks USA; we'd put a band's name and our web address on the back of each pick, and that band could buy them at cost to give out to their fans. We publicized the program on MySpace.

Band after band ordered picks customized with their names and endorsed by Hot Picks. We must have had 300 to 400 bands at the height. They would take pictures of themselves with their picks and upload them to their MySpace pages, stating that Hot Picks endorsed them. So our logo was on their pages, and when their friends clicked on it, the link would direct them to our page. It was great!

Then, we sweetened the pot. We ran a Favorite Band contest for the bands we endorsed. We gave them a banner to put on their MySpace page that had a photo of their band and a link to our page. We ran the contest once a month for over a year, nominating 10 bands each month. The band that got the most votes was featured in our ad in a national magazine (*Guitar World* or *Revolver*). These bands read those magazines and wanted to be there. In order to vote, the band's MySpace friends had to become our MySpace friends. That enabled us to communicate and market directly to the fans.

People voted like crazy! Fans would leave comments on our site about why they loved a particular band. We had this whole community talking and interacting. Both the bands and fans posted photos of themselves with Hot Picks all over MySpace.

One of the reasons our MySpace campaign worked so well is that we went after the right audience. Trying to sell mohair sweaters to the heavy metal crowd would never have worked. Selling skull and monster guitar picks to heavy metal bands and their fans was a perfect fit.

The other thing we did right was to make the campaign about the bands and their fans, not about us. In our ads, the photo of the band took prominence; we put a small photo of a Hot Pick in the corner and our website and phone number on the bottom.

We also hired someone who was part of that world to be our voice on MySpace, to interact with the bands and fans. Her name was Carlin, and she was into goth and heavy metal. I remember thinking, *They have no idea two 50-year-old guys are behind this!*

Of course, we genuinely loved all those bands and people, and I think they sensed that. Helping them helped us build a community and demand for our products. When I left the company, we had almost 20,000 MySpace friends, a veritable army of loyal consumers who loved our products. That helped us get distributors and into a lot of stores.

Mobile Marketing: Here, There, Everywhere

Mobile marketing is delivering marketing messages to consumers through their personal mobile devices, such as smartphones and iPads. The same marketing etiquette that applies to social media marketing applies to mobile marketing. It's just a way to connect with your customers—anywhere, any time.

The different forms of mobile marketing include:

Short Message Service (SMS), for sending and receiving text messages to and from mobile phone networks

MMS (Multimedia Message Service), for sending and receiving short messages of "rich content"—text, images, videos, and audios—to and from mobile subscribers

Proximity Systems, for SMS or MMS messaging to and from mobile phone subscribers in a specific geographic area

Quick Response (QR) Code, a two-dimensional bar code that can be scanned using mobile devices (with QR Readers), enabling subscribers to hyperlink to the brand's website. You can include

QR Codes in your mobile messages, social media posts, e-mails, product packaging, advertising, store displays, signage, flyers, and so on. You can generate a QR Code using a free download-able QR generator such as BeQRious (http://www.beqrious .com) and ShareSquare (http://www.getsharesquare.com).

Mobile marketing is a great way to offer rewards, discounts, premiums, detailed information on your product, exclusive access to content-rich pages on your site, and whatever other way you can think of to get your target audience excited about you and your product.

You can hire someone to develop your mobile app for you or make your own with one of the do-it-yourself sites such as AppMakr (http://www.appmakr.com). Be aware that some mobile device companies, such as Apple, will not sell apps that are purely promotional in their stores.

Rewards: A Little Goes a Long Way

Every major brand has a rewards program. Coke does, Hallmark does, Seventh Generation does, Xbox does. Why? Because they work! At Hot Picks, when we filled orders I always threw in a couple of extra picks in the package to show my love. Each pick cost only a couple of pennies. We made posters people could put up. We sold picks to garage bands at cost, so they could use them as promotional giveaways to their fans. We ran Favorite Bands contests, with the prize being free publicity in our print ads.

Find your own ways to reward your customers. Give people an incentive to demonstrate how much they like your product. Show them you appreciate the acknowledgment by giving them a freebie, a premium, a discount, or a simple thank-you. It's these little extras that make a brand experience fantastic.

Trade Shows: Create a Buzz and Leads

Exhibiting at trade shows and product expos isn't cheap or easy. But when you're the new kid on the block with a new product you need to get into the marketplace, doing so can really pay off. It gives you access to retail buyers, vendors, industry leaders, and media professionals who report on your industry. It enables you to showcase, demonstrate, and test your products on the marketplace. It allows you to scope out your competition, and it teaches you a lot about your product, your niche, and your industry.

Here are some tips for minimizing the cost and maximizing the benefit of exhibiting at trade shows:

- Choose the right show. Research trade shows catering to your category and industry.
- Get the exhibitor's registration kit, and find out who's exhibiting and attending. Talk to past participants and industry insiders.
- If two or more great trade shows are being held that year, attend the one nearest to you.
- Reserve a small booth near a big player that is likely to draw a lot of traffic.
- Find out if the show's organizer has a special section or is doing any promotions for new products. If so, get in on that action. You must contact the event organizer early to get this type of deal.
- Share a booth with another business that has a product that complements yours, but is not competition. This is a great way to lower your costs. Hot Picks found someone through a trade magazine.
- Publicize your participation in the show *before* the show. Invite potential retailers and distributors to visit your booth, and give them an incentive to do so, such as offering discounted wholesale prices.
- Make your own booth. Most events provide a covered table and a couple of chairs. Jazz the setting up with a banner, a slide show or video, and your product. If your product is small, take a professional-quality photo and have it blown up into a poster.
- Include your brand name, tag line, logo, web address, and QR code on your banner, posters, signs, flyers, business cards, and any other handouts.
- Transport and set up your own booth, if possible, to save on shipping and related costs.

- Bring plenty of business cards and a handout (sheet, flyer, or card) focused on the benefits of your product. Make the promo piece small and professional; otherwise, it will be thrown away. We gave out cards showing Hot Picks' product line and giving a little information on the company, which included contact information.
- Keep the front of your booth open and inviting. Set up your table(s) at the back and/or side(s) of the booth, not across the front. If you have a small booth, you can conduct sales in the aisle in front of it. Doing this allows you to considerably expand your booth size.
- Prepare and practice your "elevator speech (your one-line statement about the benefits of your product)." Everyone working your booth should be able to clearly articulate what your product is, who it's for, the value it provides, and what your company is about in less than three minutes.
- Get volunteers to work the booth with you. You want to be able to talk one-on-one with prospects and to leave the booth to walk the show, which is impossible to do if you're alone. Make sure the volunteers present the right image, and can discuss your product and answer any questions clearly and accurately.
- Give away something remarkable. If your product is inexpensive to produce, give away samples. Some products are too expensive to give away, though. In that case, find a clever but inexpensive giveaway that stands out. It's even better if you can put your logo and web address on it and it somehow ties in with your product.
- Walk the show. Check out competitors, vendors, distributors, and other industry professionals. Introduce yourself, show an interest in other people, ask questions, shake hands, and exchange business cards.
- Stop traffic and create a buzz. Do something that gets people's attention, draws them into your booth, and gets them thinking and talking about you. It might be a contest, a game, a raffle, a celebrity, an off-the-wall product demonstration (like the food blender company that blends two-by-fours and other weird stuff)—whatever works.

- Focus on generating leads. Don't go to a trade show expecting to leave with a pile of orders. You might get some, but most buyers don't make purchasing decisions on the fly. Instead, try to connect with potential retailers and distributors. Engage them in conversation, talk about their business, and begin to build those relationships.
- Follow up with potential customers, vendors, and other people you connected with at the show. Reach out with a brief e-mail or phone call, along with any promised product samples or media kits within a week.

At our first trade show, we gave out Hot Picks with our web address printed on the back. People of all ages, as well as musicians, rushed to get theirs. We gave out so many, it created a mob! At one point, the buyers couldn't get to us, which made them want us even more. We called it "feeding the pigeons." We created a frenzy of demand, and the buyers bought into it—and ordered our product.

BEST OF SHOW

Hot Picks won best of show two years in a row in the small accessory category at NAMM [National Association of Music Merchants, the largest music products trade show in North America]. I am so proud of those two awards. Jimmy Dunlop once told me that he has been selling guitar picks for 30 years, and I don't think he's ever won a best of show. He had a huge booth upstairs. We had a 10-by-10 booth downstairs. It was so small we had to conduct our meetings in the aisles, but we had a great product, and we found creative ways to get attention, build relationships, and promote our products.

Get the Word Out on a Limited Budget

Public relations (PR) is doing something newsworthy and getting the media to share it with their readers, viewers, and/or listeners. It's a way to promote your brand in magazines, newspapers, television, radio, and the Internet without paying for advertising. The key word here is "newsworthy," meaning, you have to do and say something of interest to the target audience. Bloggers, journalists, editors, and producers are always looking for stories that will engage, resonate with, and somehow benefit their followers. But they have no interest in yet another announcement about yet another new product and yet another new company.

You need to feed the media a fresh story angle that focuses on the *why* (value) of what you're doing, rather than just on *what* you're doing. It also needs to be current; old news is not news. To pique interest, your story had better be relevant to the audience. Don't send everyone the same plain-vanilla press release; tailor it to fit the individual publication, show, blog, or website.

Tools of the Trade

A *press release* is the main tool used for alerting the media to whatever news you want to share. It's basically a one- or two-page news story, written in third person and from an objective perspective. It should have a short and catchy headline, and the lead paragraph should hook the editor's interest and succinctly spell out the who, what, where, and when of your story. The rest of the release should spell out the why— what makes whatever you're touting so special to the target audience.

A *pitch letter* (or *query letter*) is a one-page business letter that presents a compelling story line, or hook, relating to your brand. It should pique the interest of the reporter, producer, blogger, or other media professional and point out the main bones of the story. Most important, it should provoke the person who received the submission to share the story with his or her audience.

Every press release and pitch letter should be well written and free of grammatical, spelling, and typographical errors. It should include the date of the release and your logo, website, and contact information.

A *media kit* provides a media professional with the basic information he or she needs to determine whether to move forward with your story. It typically includes a cover letter, a press release and/or pitch letter, a *backgrounder* (a short history of your company that includes a brief bio on the inventor-entrepreneur), a product sheet or flyer, a photo of you, and a photo of your product. Depending on the type of media being contacted, the kit may also include a DVD, CD, or MP3 file.

These days, most media professionals prefer an electronic media kit—files they can download from your website or that you can e-mail to them as attachments. Some people want hard copies, though, so have a few made up, and place your PR materials in an attractive folder that has your logo, website, and contact information printed on a label affixed to the front of the folder.

A well-prepared media kit makes a good first impression and tells your story—who you are, what you do, why people should care—in a concise and professional way.

Submitting Releases and Pitches

You can hire a publicist or PR agency to submit (distribute) your press releases and pitch letters; they can also write them (and will want to). But those services tend to be expensive, and they can't guarantee your story will get published, posted, or produced. I think you can do it yourself.

Do some homework to identify all the media sources that might be interested in your brand. I suggest creating a master list of all the consumer magazines, trade journals, blogs, radio programs, and TV programs that cater to your target audience and/or industry. You may also want to include on your master list a *newswire* service, such as Associated Press (http://www.ap.org), Newswire Today (http://www .newswiretoday.com), and Digg (http://www.digg.com). Some newswire services offer free press release distribution in addition to services and tools they sell.

When you create a new press release or pitch letter, identify additional media sources that might be interested in that particular story. Let's say, for example, your product is a line of plush toys and you want to publicize a photo contest you're holding in which parents submit photos of their kids with your product. In addition to sending your release to the usual contacts on your master list, you might also send it to media sources catering to parents and photographers.

Another strategy is to find a reporter or producer who is looking for people to interview or include in an article or media segment they're working on. If you have something to offer, even if it's not directly related to your product or company, it's a way to plug your brand. You can search for such opportunities on sites such as HARO (Help a Reporter Out; http://www.helpareporter.com), Media Kitty (http://www.mediakitty.com), and ProfNet (http://www.profnet.com).

Today, so many people and businesses use e-mail to communicate, you should learn how to use it effectively. Make sure to have a subject line in your e-mail message that will invite a producer or reporter to read it. We were able to get Spinformation on *The Doctors* (CBS) by using the e-mail subject line, "Thousands of children overdose on medication, and this can stop it."

To get started, check all the magazines, journals, and newsletters for your industry to see which ones have sections or special issues for "new products." Then send them a great release!

TIP

SIX SURE-FIRE WAYS TO MAKE NEWS

There are so many newsworthy things you can do to get some media attention for your brand. Here are a few to consider:

1. **Win awards.** Enter contests that recognize product innovation and best or notable new products in your product category or industry. If you win, even if it's just an honorable mention, announce it to the world. I've been awarded Product of the Year in Canada for AccuDial and Soyu Teas as well as two Edison Awards. I went up against the giants! Other companies that have received those awards include Ford, Nike, and Coca-Cola. Search for these opportunities on the Internet. Some contests require an entry fee, so use your judgment.

2. **Hold a contest.** You could hold a photo or video contest of people using your product by landmarks all over the globe. Or a jingle-writing contest. Or a "You know you're a [*name or type of product*] lover when you _____" contest. The possibilities for

customer contests are endless. Make it fun, give away prizes, and share entries and winners on your website and social media pages.

3. **Be a sponsor.** Sponsor an event or team whose audience might be interested in your product. Through our advertising in *Guitar World* we were able to become a sponsor of the Winter X Games. We gave away free products at some events and even had a booth.

4. **Use the power of free product.** We were able to exchange guitar picks for advertising space in national magazines such as *Revolver* and *Fangoria*. Similarly, we gave Jones Soda free picks in exchange for signage and sponsorship of X Games and trade shows. Obviously, if your product has a high cost, this idea is limited, but bartering free product for exposure is a good way for startups to get media and consumer exposure.

5. **Do good.** Contribute to a charitable cause or event. Volunteer, donate product for a charity auction, serve on the board, give a percentage of your profits, and/or be a spokesperson.

6. **Court celebrities.** Try to get your product in the gift bags of "red carpet" and other celebrity events. You can also send a freebie to celebrities you think will love your product. If a celebrity wears or uses your product in public, or even better, talks about it to his or her social media network or the media, it's an endorsement all their fans will notice. This type of opportunity can really work, but it usually costs a significant amount of money.

Newspapers and Magazines

First of all, you have to do your homework on the person you are trying to contact. Make sure you know his or her area of expertise (the "beat"). You don't want to send information about a kitchen gadget to a sports or political editor.

By far, the best approach is to pick up the phone and call the person you are trying to get to run a story on your product. Everyone wants a relationship. This is hard for many people to do, but it is absolutely the most effective approach. Be polite, and make your pitch quickly using your one-line benefit statement or other important and news-worthy information. Remember that these people need and want new stories—they are, after all, in the business of finding new content—but it's how you approach them that matters.

Almost all magazines have a small section devoted to new products that might interest their readers. This is the easiest way to get into a magazine. Find out who the reporter/editor is for the section your product could be included in and call him or her. Follow up with a sample of your product. Make sure you can send a high-resolution photo of your product; if you include this, the person you are in contact with at the publication company won't have to spend time and money on a photo shoot.

When you receive a call from an editor or reporter, be sure to return his or her call immediately—not tomorrow or later today, but *now*. Most editors and reporters work on deadlines; things are frequently last-minute and hectic. If the editor/reporter can't reach you quickly, your story will quickly be replaced by another to fill the editorial space that would have belonged to you. Don't lose your chance because you are too relaxed in your follow-up.

The next best way to reach the appropriate person is to contact an editor or reporter by sending information in the mail. Yes, that's right, the old-fashioned, slow U.S. Postal Service. But remember that this person gets a lot of queries all the time. What can you do to make yours stand out? I packed my guitar picks so they spilled out when the package was opened. Some people send a gift basket or gift box, which is likely to get opened. Be creative!

As a last resort, you can e-mail the editor or reporter. But only do this if the publication's website says it accepts electronic queries and submissions. Do not pester someone who does not want to be bothered; that will do nothing more than push him or her away. Instead, use an incredibly catchy subject heading that will pique the person's interest enough that he or she actually opens your e-mail and reads it.

Blogs

Find bloggers who are writing about topics that are relevant to your product. Don't be pushy, and don't try to promote your brand. Instead, contribute to the conversation, providing helpful information or insight. Offer to be interviewed by the blogger, and if the blogger takes you up on the offer, show your appreciation with some kind of gift or other reward. Invite the blogger to review your product. Bloggers love receiving free products! Bloggers also love to offer free gifts to their readers. You should contact them and offer free products in exchange for an interview. Some bloggers have a huge audience and could do a great job getting your product out there.

Leverage Your Expertise

Another way to use the Internet is to use your expertise in your product's category to write blogs. These blogs should not be about your product; in fact, the less often you mention your product, the better. You want to write about your category, offering tips and advice, solving problems, interviewing guests, and including anything else that will enhance your position as an industry expert. If you are seen as an expert, people will develop trust in you, and when they learn you have a product for sale, that trust will transfer to your product.

To really increase the impact of blogging, try to become a blogger on someone else's site in your category. For example, if you have a new tool, you should work hard to become a blogger on Handyman (http://www.handyman.com). You can leverage the visibility of this far-reaching audience. When you become an expert, you can use the power of the Internet for free rather than paying for advertising. Your name and your product's name will move up on search engine pages, allowing more people to find you faster.

Expose Yourself . . . on TV!

If you can get your product on television, you're guaranteed a lot of exposure. I'm not talking about selling your products on shopping channels (see Chapter 8) or advertising on TV. You need to appear as a guest or have your product featured on talk shows, news programs, and programs catering to a niche audience about specific subject areas, such as cooking, fashion, home-improvement, fitness, and so on. Remember what happened when a product was featured on *The Oprah Winfrey Show*? Sales went through the roof! The "Oprah effect" of being on any popular TV show can take you from 0 to 60 overnight!

Another type of TV show to consider is a reality show in which the inventor-entrepreneur pitches her or his idea to a panel of "judges," who may or may not help that person get to the next level, typically with funding. Currently, this includes *Shark Tank* (ABC), *Invention USA* (History Channel), and *Invention Hunters* (Food Network).

Both Leslie Haywood of Grill Charms and David Mayer of Clean Bottle appeared on *Shark Tank*. Leslie Haywood received three offers from the panel of investors; she went with Internet and technology mogul Robert Herjavec's offer for $50,000 in exchange for 25 percent equity in her company. David Mayer accepted billionaire and Dallas Mavericks owner Mark Cuban's offer of $60,000 in exchange for an 8 percent stake in Clean Bottle. Leslie and David received a lot of great exposure from being on the show, including extensive media coverage before and after the episodes aired. Leslie later appeared on the "One Minute to Millions" segment of the *Big Idea with Donny Deutsch* show. For these types of shows, you'll need to submit a short casting video and have a good prototype. Check the shows' websites for casting information.

Getting on TV is not the easiest thing in the world, but it can be done. You need to speak directly with someone who is in charge of generating content; that person is usually the show's producer or assistant producer. But how do you get that person's name? It might be on the television show's website, or you might be able to find it on LinkedIn. But the best bet is to prerecord the show, watch it later, and slow down the credits at the end. You will always find the names of the producer and any assistants listed, and you can make a note of their names from that.

I've been on *Big Idea with Donny Deutsch*, *Dr. Phil*, *ABC Money Matters*, and several other shows. The key is to have a unique story that fits the show and ties into current events. To get on the Donny Deutsch show (after watching several episodes), I created a package that literally spilled out guitar picks when opened. David Mayer submitted a video of himself walking around the Tour de France dressed in a giant water bottle suit, handing out Clean Bottles to cyclists and fans—this spectacle also aired on TV stations around the world! For the actual show, David surprised the panel by having National Basketball Association Champion and sports commentator Bill Walton make an appearance dressed in the giant water bottle suit! You have to do something memorable to create an impression.

Watch the shows you want to appear on, and check out their websites and social media pages. Understand each show's format and audience. How long is a typical segment? What is the host's interview style? How much time is a guest given to respond to each question? Who are the show's viewers? What do they care about? I was able to get AccuDial on *The Doctors* (CBS) for two reasons: (1) our product tied in with a hot topic: parents unintentionally giving incorrect doses of medication to their children, and (2) AccuDial addresses the problem with weight-based, rather than age-based, dosage charts on its labels.

I recommend starting with local stations. Being a member of the community is newsworthy in itself. Although it's not enough to get you on a show, it can help get the producer's attention. Appearing on a locally broadcast show is also a good way to get more comfortable in front of the camera before you go on national TV. My first TV appearance was on a local show in the San Francisco Bay Area years ago. It did not go well. I stammered, and my eyes were shifty. A friend thought I was awful; she called later and offered some advice. With her help and experience, I've learned to be more comfortable in front of the camera. Before the show, I decide what I'm going to say and practice, practice, practice. I get a good night's sleep and arrive early. I talk with the cameraman and crew before we start shooting, which relaxes me. I love the camera now! I'm still nervous, no matter how many times I've done it. But I look calm and sound natural.

Too many people ramble on, not understanding the need to talk in sound bites. Decide the three key points you want to make, and boil them down to concise sentences. But make sure it's how you actually talk, though; you don't want to sound like a robot. Think about the questions the host might ask and how you will answer them. Practice on family and friends and in front of a mirror; videotape yourself. What's your best angle? Are you smiling? Maybe you should stop doing that twitch thing. Are you talking too slow or too fast? Enunciating clearly? Constantly saying "um," "uh," "like," or "you know"? Be enthusiastic! Who doesn't love enthusiasm?

Make sure to find out what type of clothing to wear. Bring extra clothes to offer alternatives. Choose a color that complements your skin tone and hair color and that won't wash you out or be too bright under the glaring TV lighting. All white, all black, loud stripes, and busy patterns are usually a no-no. Ask if you can bring product samples and photographs of your product, and find out what format those photos should be in—traditional or high resolution (easier to film). Bring more than one of everything and always send it ahead of time to increase the chances of your product being shown.

I also offer questions ahead of time to the person interviewing me. Most people I work with love this because it makes their job easier, and obviously, it is good for you because you know the points you'd like to make!

Be Heard . . . on the Radio

Radio programs are always looking for people to interview. I like radio a lot, because you can be interviewed from the comfort of your home. With all the local stations, national, satellite, and Internet radio programs out there, you also have a lot of options. The trick is to find the right ones for you. The easiest way to do that is to do a web search for the type of radio program and topic you're interested in. To find radio programming you are interested in, you can search online directories such as NewsLink (http://www.newslink.org), RadioRow (http://www.radiorow.com), and BlogTalkRadio (http://www.blogtalkradio.com).

Again, if you're lucky enough to be chosen to be interviewed or to speak on radio, do your homework. Radio needs high energy and short answers with clear and clever language. Remember, your audience can only hear you, not see your product, so your words have to be thought about ahead of time. You will want to practice keeping your answers short, thoughtful, and oriented to the audience of that particular radio show.

Submit your story to a radio producer with a customized pitch letter. When being interviewed by phone, always use a landline in a quiet space that is free of distractions. Be yourself, and enjoy it!

Hitch Your Wagon to Someone Else's Star

A great way to quickly increase your marketing reach and clout is to get an endorsement or license from a company with a huge following in your target audience. Of course, that's often easier said than done, and it can be costly. But if you can figure out a way for a big player to benefit from teaming up with you, it may be worth your effort and money. We did it twice at Hot Picks, and both times it paid off in spades!

The first year we attended NAMM, we shared a booth with another company. It was downstairs in a less heavily trafficked area. But we managed to make a commotion by giving out Hot Picks like candy. That's what drew the product manager of B.C. Rich to our booth. His name was Rock, and he wanted some of our picks, too! B.C. Rich makes badass guitars that appeal to the heavy metal and punk rock crowds, and the company has been around forever. Knowing our picks were perfect for its customers, I got Rock's card and called him soon after the show.

I made a proposal: "How great would it be if you could pack our guitar picks in the case with your guitars?" We'd give B.C. Rich the picks for free in exchange for an endorsement. Rock said yes! But when he told me how many picks he'd need, it came out to $13,000 worth. That was a lot of money for a startup, but I knew the result would be worth it. So we did it. "The official guitar pick of B.C. Rich guitars" and "www.HotPicksUSA.com" were printed on the back of each pick. We also ran ads with photos of B.C. Rich guitars in national magazines, which the company loved. Doing so gave us credibility throughout the industry. We became bigger and bigger. The next year, our products were all over the B.C. Rich booth at NAMM.

By then, we had a lot of different designs geared to the heavy metal and goth crowds: skulls, zombies, crazy clowns, demons, and so on. But I knew we'd run out of content sooner or later.

So I went to a licensing trade show in New York City, hoping to learn how we might license another brand's images to print on our guitar picks. I felt like I had landed on another planet! The booths were so crowded I couldn't even step into them. I managed to get into some booths, and I collected a lot of business cards. I came away thinking I wanted to license brands that were known worldwide and appealed to the heavy metal crowd, like images from horror movies such as *Friday the 13th*.

When I got back to the office, I started calling companies. I didn't have much luck until I called Disney. There's nothing like starting at the top! I asked for someone in the licensing department, and a very kind person answered the phone. I said to him, "I'm just calling to ask some questions. Do you have any time to help me?" I assumed Disney was way too big for us. I didn't even know what it would take, other than a lot of money. I was used to licensing my ideas to companies, not licensing a brand from a company.

Because I was learning and not selling, the licensing rep eventually asked me what I did. I told him, and I could tell he was interested. For one thing, Disney didn't have a licensee selling guitar picks with Disney images. After we talked a little more, he asked, "How would you like to become a Disney licensee?" I almost fell out of my chair! I've always loved Disney. But the rep had some tough questions. How many stores were we currently in? We were in a lot of stores, maybe more than one thousand. What were our sales revenues? What were our forecasts? How many Disney picks did we think we could sell?

So I put together a forecast of how much I thought we could sell in year one, year two, and year three. I thought long and hard about that. If I made the minimum guarantees too high, we might not be able to meet them. If I made them too low, Disney might not be interested.

The minimum guarantee ended up being in the mid-five figures range over three years, and the royalty was a little more than 10 percent. That seemed reasonable to me; they didn't need the guarantee upfront, and it gave us the worldwide exclusive on guitar picks with Disney images for three years! I'm proud to say we made the minimum guarantees and sold a lot of picks.

When we went to NAMM, we had Disney on one side of our booth and heavy metal on the other. We had guitar picks for everyone.

Teaming up with Disney and B.C. Rich gave us incredible leverage. Coupled with our popularity on MySpace, it opened so many doors for us. It allowed us to get distributors, which got us into big chains such as Walmart and 7-Eleven, even gas stations, and that led to our first endorsement from a big-name musician.

One morning, a guy named Scott Swift noticed our picks on the checkout counter of a gas station in Nashville. He thought it would be a great promotional item for his daughter, an up-and-coming country musician. So he called us and ordered picks with a lenticular image of his daughter, Taylor Swift, on them. That year, Taylor won many awards, including four Grammys. Her songs were topping the country and pop charts, her records were selling in the millions, she was appearing on TV and in concerts all over the world, and she was giving Hot Picks to her fans! We became a licensee, and we sold a *lot* of Taylor Swift picks.

• • •

You don't have to have a big idea and spend lots of money on marketing to play this game and win it. All it takes is a simple idea that people want and the ability to connect with people, build relationships, and deliver on your promises.

8

Winning and Losing at Retail

EVERYONE WANTS to know how to get his or her product into stores—the more stores the better. I think the best way to win at retail is to start with small orders from a few local and regional stores, and add accounts and volume slowly. For one thing, the big stores only want products they know will sell, and often the only way to convince them of that is to have a product that is selling well in smaller stores. The other thing is that rarely does a product hit all the marks when it first arrives on the market. Usually, something isn't quite right. Maybe the price is too high or too low. Perhaps the packaging isn't effective. The product might be targeted at the wrong audience. Or maybe the product itself needs to be altered.

You absolutely *will* need to make changes to your product based on what you learn after you bring it to market. That is why I feel strongly about manufacturing in the United States and doing small production runs, so you can make those changes quickly and not get stuck with inventory you can't sell. If you order too much product and there's something wrong with it, you're going to incur a loss. Think of your first few retail experiences as a form of test marketing, a way not only to sell product and build brand recognition, but also to find out what works and what doesn't work. If a store doesn't want your product, ask why. Staying in communication with the buyer, manager, or owner of each store gives you a chance; keep track of how your product is selling, and ask for feedback on who's buying your product and on anything you might be able to do to increase sales. Then, you can make an informed decision about whether and how to change your pricing, packaging, and/or product.

At Hot Picks, we had to fine-tune both our product and our packaging after bringing our product to market. As I mentioned earlier, independent music stores weren't interested in our initial "hot chicks" designs because those products did not appeal to their core clientele. When I was able to get 7-Eleven interested in our picks, they didn't like our packaging because the clamshells weren't sealed. Shoplifters could grab the clamshells, take out the picks, and put the empty package back. Shoppers also couldn't see all the picks in each clamshell. We learned that a lot of other stores wouldn't accept our product packaged that way, either. We had to change the packaging, even though unsealed clamshells were relatively cheap and custom packaging would cost a lot. We realized a rotary pack (in which each pick in the package could be individually seen) would be better, because people could see what they were buying and couldn't remove the picks from the pack and steal them as easily as they could with clamshells. The new packaging showed the value beautifully and helped us get into 7-Eleven and later into Walmart. But the big players wouldn't have given us the time of day if we hadn't first tested our product on local stores, ironed out some of the bugs, and got some traction in the market. By the time I started knocking on the doors of national chains and megastores, we'd already sold a lot of Hot Picks.

Another way to test the market and get some additional sales under your belt is to set up an online store on your website and sell directly to consumers. Just make sure to solicit feedback from your online customers and to reward them for it, and never give them a better price than they could get at a retail store. Retailers don't want to compete with you.

Selling your product to a company once is not difficult. The trick is to get repeat sales; then you really know you are in business. Repeat sales come from doing a few test orders on the right retailers and tweaking your product, packaging, and/or price point based on what you have learned from those sales. When you have that right mix, you'll get repeat sales.

Continue to learn and adjust as you add more stores. Once you've found the formula that works, it is easy to replicate on a larger scale. When your product is selling well in local, regional, and smaller stores, as well as through your own online store, it is much easier to get your product into bigger retailers. If your product sells, stores will order it again and again.

Start Local, Go National, Grow Global

I knew our Hot Picks should be in 7-Eleven early in the game. It didn't matter to me that everyone I knew thought I was nuts. "Why would a national convenience store carry guitar picks?" my family, friends, and colleagues would ask. "Do a lot of musicians visit those locations?" Maybe. I didn't know. What I did know from studying the market and from our experiences at NAMM and on MySpace was that the people who loved our picks—young people who were huge fans of heavy metal music and the lifestyle as a whole—shopped at 7-Eleven. Kids go into convenience stores day in and day out. Our picks had become more like a collectible or novelty gift item than simply a tool used to play the guitar. We had so many designs, and our packaging was cool. The price point was very affordable, especially compared with other items in the store. I thought selling our picks at convenience stores would work perfectly. But how was I going to get into 7-Eleven?

If I had walked into the corporate office of 7-Eleven in Texas and proposed my plan, I would have been shown the door immediately. They would have thrown me out! Instead, I went down to my neighborhood 7-Eleven, a store I hadn't regularly frequented, and introduced myself as a local customer. The store wasn't very busy, so I asked to speak to the manager. The owner of the franchise, a very nice older man, came out to talk with me.

"I'm a local businessman with a product that's selling in a lot of stores, and I have a hunch you could sell a lot of them in your store, too," I said. When I showed him the picks, I could tell he was skeptical. He had a few toys and novelty items in the store, but 7-Eleven primarily sells snacks and drinks. Prior to this meeting, I had put Hot Picks in a few other local 7-Elevens. We'd gotten a bit of traction, so I had a good feeling about it. We'd learned how to price them and had built a display to promote them.

The store owner wasn't convinced. He didn't think it was a good fit. But, I made a deal with him. I asked him to put my display on his counter for a week and keep 100 percent of the proceeds for whatever sold. I just wanted to know if my hunch was right, and that our picks would sell in this retail environment. He said okay, and brought in the store manager. She was not happy about putting my display on the prime real estate by the cash register. I sensed she'd be a problem, but she put the Hot Picks display on the counter.

I told a couple of people about it in the office. A couple of days later, someone in my office told me he had gone down to the 7-Eleven to see how sales were going, but the display was gone. I thought the office manager might have taken them down, because I knew she wasn't on board with the idea. I went back to the store supposing they hadn't done well, but I still wanted to know what had happened. How many had sold? To whom? When? What did people say? I wanted any information I could get to help me with my market research.

The manager saw me walk in, and looked at me oddly. I walked over to her and asked, "How'd we do?"

"We sold out!" she said. "We'd sold out in two days!"

It was at that moment that I knew the price point, packaging, and design were going to work for the specific retail environment my product was in.

I gave the store more products to sell. Not long after that, I got a call from the regional sales manager asking about our picks. He had heard about a product that had sold out in one of their stores in just a weekend! Could we meet? He was very kind. He said, "Steve, I would never have thought in a million years that 7-Eleven would be the right store to carry this product. But you're right; it is! We're selling a lot of them."

The regional sales manager wanted to do another test. Maybe he thought my friends were going down to the store and buying our picks (and I didn't blame him if he did, for the simple reason that guitar picks were not the typical commodity being sold in 7-Eleven stores). So we put them in 10 more stores. I built the displays, packed them up, and sent them to the stores he had selected. Sure enough, the same thing happened. We went from 10 stores to 100, to meeting the corporate heads for 7-Eleven, all in a short period of time. We eventually had broad distribution in 7-Elevens throughout the United States.

We actually ended up selling Hot Picks at retailers worldwide; our international sales were a good portion of our business. We found our international distributors through trade shows. You definitely need distributors to get your product into retailers that are not based in your home country, and trade shows are the best way I know to find them. You can also check with trade associations, ask for referrals from companies that are selling product overseas, and search the Internet.

Here are a few things we learned from selling Hot Picks all over the world:

- Stores outside the United States are usually smaller than within the country. They have limited shelf space.
- Retailers outside North America are more price-sensitive. Where U.S. retailers like to put a large number of picks in a package, retailers elsewhere wanted smaller packages to reduce the price and the shelf space required. Your distributor will help you with pricing and packaging issues.
- International distributors place big orders. The thing that was great about international distributors is that they would order a couple of months' worth of stock.
- The distributors frequently demand discounts. We found that they sometimes used the discount to do co-op marketing with their retailers.
- International shipments usually cost more than our U.S. shipments; if you are dealing with an international shipper, be sure you allow and plan for that extra cost.
- Shipping overseas can be very difficult and stressful. Find a freight forwarder to help you. We used Concordia to ship our products overseas. The shippers would pick up from our ware-

house and deliver to our customers. The freight forwarder handled all the paperwork, and we had products selling in Japan, Germany, the United Kingdom—all around the world.

- Theft and shrinkage are big problems. We realized we needed to pack up our product in such a way as to prevent these two things from happening. Your freight forwarder will help you decide the best way to handle this.

Start local and small and proceed slowly: Gradually add accounts. Wait until you're ready before going after big stores. Expand your distribution from local, to national, to international when and as you are able. If you can accomplish this, you can win at the retail game without losing your shirt or your sanity.

How to Get Your Product into Retail Stores

In the United States alone, there are 1.5 million retail stores selling $2.5 trillion dollars' worth of products each year. That's amazing; the opportunities are huge! The challenge is being able to place your product in the right stores.

In Chapter 3, I showed you how to study the market to find potential merchants for your product. That exercise began with determining which consumer groups might buy your product and being able to identify the retail stores where those people shop. The next step was determining the different types of retailers that are currently selling your product category (e.g., independent music stores, chain stores, big-box mass market stores, superstores, and convenience stores) then identifying all the different stores within each retail category.

At this point in the game, it's time to decide which stores you're going to go after first and how you're going to do that. I suggest starting with independently owned stores in your area and working your way up to regional chains, second- and third-tier national chains, and big national (and perhaps later, international) chains, big-box stores, and superstores.

There are three ways to get your product into stores:

1. Peddle your product to retailers yourself.
2. Find one or more distributors to carry your product.
3. Hire a manufacturer's representative to sell your product to retailers for you.

Do It Yourself

A buyer is going to decide whether to carry your product in a particular store. Buyers know which products work for their store and their shoppers, which products sell well at specific times of the year, as well as which trends are waning and which ones are emerging in their market. The buyers' job is to make sure the right products are purchased at the right time, at the right prices, and in the right quantities so that the merchandise desired by customers is in stock, but doesn't just sit there. It has to sell!

Retail buyers are always looking for products. They constantly check out other stores to see what's selling and what's new. If you start small and gain some traction in the marketplace, buyers will take notice and you may start receiving calls from chain stores.

In the beginning, though, it's all on your shoulders to seek out buyers and make those calls. In fact, you (or someone else in your company) will probably always handle at least some accounts, even if you hire a manufacturer's rep and get a distributor. Most manufacturer's

COVERING ALL THE BASES
Craig Wolfe/CelebriDucks

Our distributors have their own sales reps, and we have had manufacturer's reps over the years, with varying degrees of success. But reps represent a lot of different brands, and the bigger companies with bigger lines get most of their attention because there's more profit potential for them. We're still not a huge company, so we don't expect reps to give us that kind of attention. It's amazing how many ducks we've sold on our own. And I make a lot of the calls myself.

reps aren't interested in selling to small stores. Most distributors don't sell at all; they just take orders. So, if the store you want doesn't buy from your distributor or isn't big enough for your manufacturer's rep to bother with, you'll have to pitch your product to the retail buyer yourself. After all, who knows and loves their product better and is a better representation of the brand?

Finding a Buyer

So how do you find a buyer? When you call a retail store, ask to speak to the buyer or someone who makes purchasing decisions. Doing so will save you a lot of time and effort. It's also important to call at a time when the person you are trying to reach is not very busy. Typically, the best times to call are Tuesday morning before the daily grind begins, or after work ends for the day. Calling on a Monday or Friday is never a good idea. Most people spend Monday prioritizing projects that need to be completed during the week, and Friday is typically spent wrapping things up and focusing on the weekend. Learn to allocate your time in a way that benefits your business but also benefits the time constraints of your contacts who will ultimately help promote your company.

With small retailers, the buyer is often the store owner or store manager. Sometimes, you'll be able to speak with the buyer the first time you call, so be prepared to pitch your product during that initial call.

With larger retailers, it's not as easy to reach the buyer. Whoever answers the phone is not going to give up the buyer's name, so you're going to have to find it yourself. Keep in mind that bigger stores have different buyers for specific product categories and/or certain geographic areas. Once you have the name of the right buyer, it will probably take you several tries and a long time before you actually speak to him or her—if you ever get that chance. Sometimes, the only way to get into a big chain is with a manufacturer's rep.

Here are some ways to find retail buyers:

Trade shows. I think trade shows are the number one way to find retail buyers outside your local area. Tradeshows are a great opportunity to meet not only retailer buyers, but also regional, national, and international distributors and manufacturer's reps. In fact, we found all of our international distributors and our Walmart manufacturer's rep at trade shows, but you can't get a list of retail buyers attending the show. As an attendee or exhibitor, you can get a list of other exhibitors, but not attendees. To find and meet buyers, you've got to walk the floor, talk to people, and shake some hands. There's a trade show for every industry. NAMM, the big music industry show, is held twice a year. The premier toy fair is held annually in New York City. You can find trade shows at the Trade Shows News Network (TSNN) website (http://www.tsnn.com).

Mailing lists. Find and purchase a mailing list of retailers for a specific type of store (e.g., convenience stores) or for a specific industry and/or region. Such lists provide the buyer's name, specialty/region (if applicable), and contact information. When I was working with Hot Picks, I bought a mailing list of every music store in the United States. Make sure the list is up-to-date. Stores go in and out of business, so these lists become outdated and unusable rather quickly. Find a list that's less than a year old, and make sure the mailing list company has a good reputation.

Retail store directories. Directories such as Chain Store Guide (http://www.chainstoreguide.com), TheSalesmanGuide.com (http://www.thesalesmanguide.com), and Monday Report on Retailers (http://www.mondayreport.ca) provide basic information, including buyer names, for various retail outlets. These are usually available as downloadable lists or online databases; some are also available as printed books and on disks. You will most likely have to pay for access to the database or purchase the downloadable file, CD, or book. Again, be wary of any directory you buy. Make sure it's current and you trust the company.

Showrooms. There are permanent showrooms for different product categories all across the United States where buyers go to find products for their stores. They are like shopping malls for retailers. When I had my Softies early in my career, that is how I found my mentor, Steve Askin, at his toy and novelty gift showroom in Los Angeles, called What's New. Here are the websites of a few showrooms: L.A. Mart (http://www.lamart.com), AmericasMart (http://www.americasmart.com), 7 W New York (http://www.7wnewyork.com), World Market Center Las Vegas (http://www.wmclv.com), and Dallas Market Center (http://www.dallasmarketcenter.com). To find more, just do a web search for "wholesale showrooms."

Referrals. Ask other manufacturers in your industry how they got into retail stores. They may be willing to give you the names of buyers with whom they deal. Your contract manufacturer might also be able to give you the names of buyers. For Hot Picks, I looked at the advertisements in *Guitar World* and formed relationships with other manufacturers in the industry. I just picked up the phone and asked who they dealt with. If I wasn't in direct competition with their products, they told me how to get in. They were very helpful. Companies that are already successful are usually willing to share.

Social media. If you're a LinkedIn member, you can search for retail buyers in your industry or product category or for a particular store. For example, several buyers for Kmart are on LinkedIn (http://www.linkedin.com/title/buyer/at-kmart).

One way or another, get the name(s) of the buyer(s) responsible for purchasing your product category in the store(s) you're going after. He or she is the person you need to speak with—unless you have an "in" with a high-level executive who can directly connect you to the buyer.

Pitching to Retail Buyers

Your first contact with the buyer should be over the phone, not by e-mail or snail mail. The premier contact is meeting a buyer face-to-face at a trade show or other industry event and following up with a

MAKING A VALUE PROPOSITION THEY CAN'T REFUSE
David Mayer/Clean Bottle

We did a big promotion at Tour de France, where I dressed up like a giant Clean Bottle and ran around, handing out product, and getting on international TV every day. Before the race, we reached out to all the independent bike shops, told them about the promotion, and said, "We're going to have 100,000 people going to our website and wanting this bottle. They won't want to pay $8 for us to ship them a $9.99 bottle. So we have a store locator on our site, where people can find a store near them. If you buy 200 bottles for $100, we'll give you free shipping and put a link to your store on our Store Locator page. So people will go to your store to buy the bottle, and while they're in your store, maybe they'll also buy a bike helmet or accessory, or maybe a $3,000 bike! Suddenly, the value proposition went from making $5 on every $10 bottle they sold to also getting secondary advertising via our Tour de France stint—which, by the way, we filmed and posted on our site and on YouTube—and getting people into their stores to see whatever else they might want to buy then or later.

phone call. Never send a packet of information without first talking with the buyer and clearing the way to send it.

If you're lucky, you'll have the buyer's direct line, and he or she will answer the first time you call. More than likely, you will need to be persistent. Never leave a voicemail. The person you are calling will never call you back. You are selling; the other person is buying.

You might be transferred to an assistant buyer, who does a lot of work for the buyer and will be a buyer someday, too. Talking with assistant buyers is not a bad thing; they can help you get to the buyers and advise you on what to say and do. They might also be able to get you into *vendor day*, an entire day many of the larger stores devote to listening to pitches from potential vendors. It's not as great as talking to the buyer directly, but, to be frank, you're never going to have a lot of time to pitch to a buyer.

It's very hard to get a buyer for one of the giants, such as Walmart, on the phone. Even if you eventually are successful, the process to get there is arduous and the evaluation procedures are complicated and time-consuming. Keep in mind: it is much more difficult to get your product into those stores than it is to get one of their buyers on the phone. Buyers at second- and third-tier retail stores are more accessible. During my time at Hot Picks, we were able to get into a lot of chain stores, such as Hot Topic. We did this by finding the buyer's name and just picking up the phone and calling.

When you do reach a buyer, that first phone call will be short, so make it count. Be personable, professional, and to the point. Otherwise, buyers will cut you short very quickly. Introduce yourself, state why you're calling, what your product is and does, what its main benefit is (your *one-line benefit statement*), and why you think your product is a good fit for their store.

If you've piqued the buyer's interest, he or she may ask you some questions: "How many stores are you in? Which stores are you in? What are your sales volumes? Where is your product manufactured? How is it packaged? How many SKUs do you have? Do you have a barcode? Where is it warehoused? How much inventory do you carry? What are your production lead times? How long have you been in business? How do you market your product?" The buyer may not ask all these questions up front, but once interested in your product, that person will ask you a million questions. Be prepared to answer them. Ultimately, a buyer wants to know that your product will sell and that you can handle his or her business.

If the buyer doesn't ask questions or asks you to send more information, offer to send additional information by e-mail or snail mail. Send a sell sheet, flyer, or catalog page that describes your product, highlights its benefits, and has a good photograph or illustration of your product. Always send a pricing sheet. If you have a restricted-access pricing page on your website, you can give the buyer the secret code to access that page either during your phone conversation or in your packet. If the buyer has expressed a strong interest in your product, you might also send a sample product, if it's feasible and affordable to do so. (Some products are too expensive or too big to send.) Always include a one-page cover letter thanking the buyer for his or her time; referencing the phone conversation; listing several stores currently selling your product, any testimonials from other stores, any recent media coverage you've received, and any awards you've won; and providing your contact information.

Lastly, follow up and try to get the order. Make it as easy as possible for the buyer to say yes.

Buyers often want to test out a product before committing to a large order. You can offer to give them product on consignment for 30 days. If they don't sell your product within that time period, you'll take it back. I love doing this, because if the product has already been tested and I know everything is right, I can almost guarantee the product will sell. Call them back 30 days later and ask how they are doing: "What's working? What's not?" Doing this takes a lot of time, but it works. That strategy worked well for us at Hot Picks.

Another way to tantalize prospective buyers to give you the order is to offer them a money-back guarantee. If your product does not sell, you will buy it back. This *always* works. Here's another trick: when you call the store, tell the person answering that you are in the competitor's store down the street. Leverage one store against the next. People don't like to be the first, but if they know their competitor is selling your product, they are more likely to want it, too. That tactic always got them to say "yes" and carry our product.

From my experience, if you change your package and have different SKUs, you can sell to a variety of retailers from mass markets to independent stores.

Distributors

Once you get to a certain level, you might consider using a distributor. Distributors are going to take their cut, of course, but they can work wonders. You also have to realize that distributors don't sell; they simply distribute. So you have to build demand for your product first,

THE QUEEN OF COLD CALLING
Leslie Haywood/Grill Charms

My product is in small independent retailers all over the United States. I'm not in mass market retailers now, by choice. That is not to say it will never happen; the business is fluid. But when you go that route, you've got to be ready, and there's no going back. Once you're in Walmart, all those independent retailers will stop carrying your product because they don't want the same merchandise as the mass retailers. So you have to make a conscious decision whether and when to go mass market.

I enjoy where I am: in specialty retailers. I found most of them by going to the store locator pages on the websites of companies that produce a product in the same genre—for example, a steak thermometer. Chances are, stores that sell steak thermometers are a fit for Grill Charms.

Then, I just call them. I'm not afraid of talking to anybody; I'm the Queen of Cold Calling. These are fun calls. I make sure I get to the right person, and I use the same line. I say, "Hi, I'm Leslie Haywood, and this is probably going to be your craziest call of the morning. I invented a kitchen gadget, and I'd love to see if it's a good match for your store. Can I e-mail you some wholesale information?" Saying "craziest call" lightens the mood. Saying "I invented" hooks their curiosity. They want to know what this girl on the other end of the line invented, so they give me their e-mail address, I send off the information, and I'm in the door.

before a distributor will purchase large volumes of your product and sell it directly to retailers.

There is one huge distributor in the music products industry, called Kaman Music Corporation (KMC Musicorp). I thought, *If we could just get Hot Picks into Kaman, our worries would be over*! Kaman told us stores had to be asking for our product before they would be willing to jump in. If we could create demand, Kaman would fill it. Otherwise, they weren't interested. Once we created demand with our ads and social media, the customers were asking the stores for our product. That, in turn, got retailers asking their distributors for it, and then the distributors asked us for it.

Once you work with a distributor, you lose contact with the retailers—you no longer have direct relationships with them. The retailers purchase your product directly from the distributors. If your distributor decides not to work with you any longer, you might lose all of those accounts. Having a distributor is a double-edged sword that can either hurt or help you in the long run. So think carefully before going with a distributor. If you do, consider keeping your most important accounts in-house.

These are some ways to find distributors:

- Referral from your contract manufacturer, other entrepreneurs in your industry, and trade associations
- Trade shows and product fairs
- Social media networks such as LinkedIn
- Internet search
- Trade magazines (browsing advertisements and classifieds)

Manufacturer's Representatives

A manufacturer's representative (or agency) typically sells the products of several producers to retailers and wholesalers in specific product categories and geographic areas. Most sell primarily or exclusively to midsize to large retailers and wholesalers. Few sell to small retailers and to mom-and-pop shops outside major metropolitan areas. Manufacturer's reps work on a commission basis. Most charge between 5 and 10 percent of the sales they bring in; some charge as much as 25 percent. The right manufacturer's rep may be worth the cost.

A manufacturer's rep with a solid track record in your category may have the connections and expertise to get your product into big stores that otherwise wouldn't give you the time of day. At the least, he or she may be able to do it much faster. Manufacturer's reps travel a lot, visiting several companies and representing several companies at the same time, which enables them to spread their travel costs over several accounts—and reach farther than you might be able to yourself or with whatever in-house sales staff you have.

There are potential downsides to hiring a manufacturer's rep. If a rep represents bigger producers and a lot of products, he or she may not give your product the attention it deserves. Not all manufacturer's reps are created equal either; some are definitely more capable than others. So investigate any manufacturer's reps you are considering. Do some homework, and ask some questions: "What products do you represent? Who are your clients? To what retailers and wholesalers have you sold product recently? What geographic areas do you cover? What areas do you *not* cover? What is your commission rate? Does your business style and personality reflect well on your brand?"

Make sure the rep is a good fit for your product before signing a contract, and think carefully before signing an exclusive. Sometimes you can sign an exclusive for a certain amount of time or for a certain performance level. I don't give anyone exclusives at the beginning, but if they prove they can sell a certain amount, then I will. In order to keep the exclusive, they have to sell consistently.

The best way to find a reputable manufacturer's rep is to get a referral from another entrepreneur in your industry or from a retail buyer. You can also become a member of Manufacturers' Agents National Association (http://www.manaonline.org), which enables you to access its online "Rep Finder" searchable database. These are other options: Attend a trade show, where you're sure to find manufacturer's reps looking for new products to sell. Search LinkedIn. Use an online service such as RepHunter.net (http://www.rephunter.net); be aware, some of these sites charge a membership fee. You can also do a web search for "manufacturer's rep" and your product category.

On the Shelves of Giants

Not surprisingly, it takes a lot of effort and time to get into superstores, big-box stores, and huge national and international chains. They will want to see a track record of strong sales and growth. They will put

GOT GUTS? TRY MASS-RETAIL!

Nancy Tedeschi/SnapIt Eyeglass Repair Kit

I have distributors and manufacturer's reps. To find distributors, I went to stores and looked on the bottom of the packaging [of a product] to see who was distributing it. I found my reps by researching to find out which vendors were bringing in which products to the stores I was interested in. I also used LinkedIn and worked the trade shows. I found my Walgreens rep at a housewares trade show. I hired a different rep to get me into Walmart, but it didn't happen. But I found another guy who had worked for Walmart for many years and is now a rep, bringing in products, and he got me the interview. We're still negotiating, and one of the sticking points is price.

It's a real problem because I'm selling to Walgreens at one price and I want to protect the integrity of that price. I have three prices: a small retailer price, a distributor price, and a mass retailer price. I don't think it's right that somebody, even Walmart, gets it at a different price. Same thing with my reps; they all get the same commission rate.

you through a long, involved selection process that includes providing a lot of information. They may want you to change your product and/or packaging—at your expense. They will want a price that is so discounted you'll need to do some number crunching and serious analysis to determine whether you can sell a large enough volume to make it worthwhile. If and when they do place an order, it will be for a lot of product, and if sales take off, they may expect you to refill and increase that order quickly. So you had better be ready.

We used a manufacturer's representative to get Hot Picks into Walmart. A man who represented products for Walmart found us at NAMM. But it took more than just knowing him to develop our business. We still had to fill out all those vendor applications, provide an enormous amount of information, and go through a long evaluation process. It took us about three months to get approved. I don't know whether there's a way to bypass a process similar to that for giants such as Walmart.

Other Retailing Options

Brick-and-mortar stores may be the best way to sell your product to consumers, but it's not the only way. You can always sell directly to consumers at public venues such as product fairs and open-air markets or by placing mail order ads in magazines and online. But there are other types of retail merchants that have a much bigger reach and the potential for a much higher volume of sales. The three most popular and reliable are e-tailers (webstores), home shopping networks (TV), and mail order catalog companies.

E-tailers

You can purchase just about anything online now, and people are becoming more and more comfortable with shopping online. It's a great time to sell on the web, and experts predict the experience is only going to get better. There are thousands of shopping sites on the Internet—including online superstores, such as Amazon.com; open online markets, such as eBay; the online stores of brick-and-mortar chains, big-box retailers, and megastores; specialty "e-tailers" that sell only online; and, of course, the online stores of producers.

My advice is to really check out any e-tailers you're considering having sell your product. Find out whether they sell products in your category and how much they are selling every month. Find out who their vendors and customers are. Which sites are they linked to? How many visitors do they get each month? What are the terms and conditions of selling products on their site? What's their cut? Be careful, and be selective. Online shopping is a big world. Investigate each site, and make sure it is a right fit for your product. Only pursue e-tailers with the potential to sell your product, increase awareness of your brand, and be a positive reflection on your brand.

I strongly suggest that you use online selling to supplement your retail sales, not as your sole or even primary sales channel. It's a good way to reach consumers in areas where you don't have retailers and to tap into the growing online shopping market, which is expected to account for about 10 percent of all consumer shopping by 2016.

Of course, you can also have your own online store on your website. We created a Hot Picks webstore for a few reasons: It made it easy for our MySpace friends to just click to our site and buy our products right then and there. It enabled customers who didn't live near one of our retailers (we had a Store Locator page on our site, too) to purchase Hot Picks. It enabled us to make our entire product line available to customers in one place, because few of our retailers carried all of our designs all of the time.

We soon learned that just building a webstore is not enough. People have to be able to find you. So we learned about SEO and how to optimize our site for Internet searches. We couldn't afford online ads, so we loaded our site with key words that the heavy metal crowd and guitar players might use in their searches. We changed our content regularly, keeping it fresh so the web spiders (automated servers that pick up new content and add them to search engines) would constantly pick up our site. We also put our web address everywhere: on our products, packaging, catalog, brochures, trade show posters, business cards, social media pages, magazine ads, and so on.

If you decide to have your own website, please heed these words of caution:

- Use a reputable online credit card processor that many established websites use.
- Always price your products a little higher than your retailers' prices for your products. You never want your retailers to feel like they are in competition with you. Sometimes Hot Picks would run online promotions with some of the stores that carried our product to show we supported them.
- Have a Store Locator page, and prominently display it and use content to direct customers toward it. You want your retailers to

be happy, and you want customers to be able to find a retailer near them.

- Fill your online orders immediately, and personally thank your online customers for their business.

We also used Amazon.com and a few other e-tailers. If you want to sell your product on Amazon.com, you have two options:

1. You fill and ship your Amazon.com orders: Amazon.com posts your product on its site, processes the order, and pays you. You pack the order from your inventory and ship the order to the customer. Cost: a flat fee of $39.99 per month.
2. Amazon.com fills and ships your orders: You send your product to Amazon.com. It processes the order, packs and ships the order, and pays you. Cost: $1.00 per unit, plus $0.37 per pound weight per unit, plus $0.45 per cubic foot per month for storage of your product.

Hot Picks sold well online and helped our retails sales, too. But our main focus, and our bread and butter, was always our retailers.

Home Shopping Channels

Getting your product on a home shopping channel is a great way to sell a lot of product fast. A home shopping channel is a TV network dedicated to selling product direct to consumers via the television. These programs are popular not only in the United States; they are a worldwide phenomenon. Home shopping networks run 24 hours a day, 7 days a week, and feature different types of products at different times. Each product is pitched to the TV audience by the show's hosts and sometimes by the product's inventor, with the camera zooming in on the product while the hosts and sometimes happy customers talk about the exciting features and wonders of the item. To add to the excitement, there is usually a timer that shows how much longer consumers have to order the product, either by calling a toll-free number or going to the show's webstore.

A home shopping channel should not be confused with an *infomercial*. These are two very different things. An infomercial is paid advertising that is used to sell a single product or a few products direct to the consumer via mail order. Infomercials only feature the products of the company paying for the commercial, which is usually the manufacturer. Home shopping networks sell a lot of different products produced by many different companies. They are retailers; they just display and sell their products on television rather than in stores. Home shopping shows depend heavily on repeat business from customers. Customer service is everything. They are not looking to sell subpar merchandise and make a quick sale. They are looking to make customers very happy so they keep coming back.

The two biggest home shopping players currently are QVC (Quality, Value, Convenience; http://www.qvc.com) and HSN (Home Shopping Network; http://www.hsn.com). Big networks such as these do billions of dollars of business just in their U.S. divisions. That's not even counting business revenue from overseas!

The biggest upside to selling your product on a home shopping network is that you can potentially sell huge quantities in the mere minutes they give the host and/or you to pitch it. The biggest downside is that many products don't sell well, and if they don't sell, all that unsold product gets kicked right back to you. Sometimes, you get stuck in a bad time slot and they'll still ship it back to you. Other times, they will give you another chance.

Home shopping networks are looking for products that, first and foremost, demonstrate well. That's another upside of home shopping networks: it's a good way to get consumers excited about products that don't sell well in retail stores because they need to be demonstrated to show the product's features and benefits. QVC and HSN sell a wide range of product categories; you will find lists of the types of products they are looking for on their websites.

Most of these networks have a large female viewing audience. The typical customer is a suburban woman aged 35 or older, with a household income of $75,000 up to $200,000, who uses home shopping networks to buy for herself and her family and friends.

Be professional, and submit your product directly through a network's website, following the specifications given on the site. Many of these networks have vendor training and manuals. Read them and get as much help as you can to avoid making costly mistakes.

If a home shopping channel is interested in selling your product, it will want to move fast. So you need to have your manufacturing in place when you present to one. Most networks want a minimum $30,000 order (wholesale), so don't think you can ship 100 units for them to try to sell on the air.

Another thing you should know is that home shopping networks take quality very seriously. They will drop-test your product off a ladder and do just about everything else imaginable to make sure your packaging and product are top-notch. If they are not, the networks will send it all back. So be very familiar with their requirements, and make sure you meet them.

Mail Order Catalogs

Mail order catalogs may be old school—but at last count, in 2010, almost $300 trillion worth of goods were sold by mail order worldwide! Today, virtually every printed mail order catalog has an online version, and some are now available only online. Many mail order catalog companies have a huge and loyal customer base. These are just a few: Brookstone, Lands' End, Lillian Vernon, One Step Ahead, Smith & Hawken, and Spiegel.

If you can get your product in a mail order catalog with a good following, that is a relatively easy way to get more of your product out on the market. So it's worthwhile to investigate whatever mail order catalog opportunities are available for your product category. Make sure the catalog is a right fit for your product and target audience. Mail order catalogs started contacting us. One of the catalogs we were in specialized in Disney products, so it carried our Mickey Mouse guitar picks.

Creating Happy Campers and Repeat Sales

Getting your product into stores is one thing, and it's a huge thing. But getting stores to continue carrying your product is another—and it's crucial to your success and growth. You want to *add* accounts, not *replace* them. Your goal is to get stores to not only keep ordering your product but to increase the size of their orders. Your product ought to be in as many stores as possible with numerous customers asking them for your product so that other stores come calling or at least take your calls. How do you do that? By delivering great products and great customer service.

I suggest looking at your competition right away and asking yourself: "How do they ship orders? How do they treat their customers? How does their product look in the store? What are they missing, or what could be improved?" I can guarantee they are missing a connection, a one-on-one relationship, with their customers. That's how, as a smaller company, you can really shine. Big companies just can't, or won't, give that personalized customer service that adds so much value to your product and gives you so much leverage with customers.

There are a lot of ways to provide a level of customer service that will wow customers and keep them coming back for more. Here are a few surefire ways to create happy campers and repeat sales:

Answer the phone. Whatever you do, have someone available to answer your phone at all times during regular business hours. If you have retail accounts in different time zones, you may need to adjust your business hours or schedule phone or Skype meetings for when other people are available. Make sure the people who answer your phone are friendly and professional and the callers promptly get what they are looking for. That will improve your relations with all the people and companies you deal with, not just your retailers and consumers. Every call needs to be answered by a real person, whether it is from a retailer who has a question or problem or wants to start carrying your product; a consumer who wants to know where to buy or how to return your product; a charity looking for a sponsor; a journalist wanting to profile your company or interview you; or a potential investor. Also be certain the reason for the call is dealt with promptly and courteously.

Show your appreciation. Let your retailers, distributors, and consumers know you appreciate their business. Send them personal thank-you notes. Pick up the phone and say, "Thanks!" Acknowledge them in your social media posts and on your website. Reward them for their loyalty whenever and however possible, with special discounts, promotions, and gifts.

Make good on promises. Nothing annoys a customer more than being surprised by a late order, short order, or an order with broken, substitute, or defective product. Retailers and distributors want what they want, when they want it. Know what you can and can't do *before* you take the order. Don't promise what you're not sure you can deliver, and make sure your orders are filled and shipped properly and promptly. If something unforeseen happens and you can't fill an order exactly or deliver it on time, let the customer know immediately and give him or her options.

Fix it. Things go wrong, even in the most conscientious, well-run companies. When something goes awry, even if it's not your

LOSE A SALE, WIN A CUSTOMER
Annette Giacomazzi/CastCoverZ

Customer service is a key component of my business model. We want to create a fabulous experience that makes customers want to come back and pass on. We sell direct to the consumer on our online store as well as to distributors and medical professionals. Regardless of who is ordering our product, the minute the customer hits that buy button, it's their product; it's no longer mine. We make sure they understand that with every contact they have with us. If there's a problem, we say "your order" and "your product," and from the get-go we always say, "We'll take care of it," no matter what. If the U.S. Postal Service loses a shipment, that may not be my fault, but it's my responsibility. The product is the customer's at that point, but we're the stewards of their order. So we take responsibility and take care of the problem. One of my mottos, which I've made clear to my team is, we may lose the sale but we never lose a customer.

company's fault, make it right as quickly as possible. Product damaged in transit? Replace it immediately; you can collect later from the insurance company or freight carrier. Product doesn't work or the color isn't quite right? Replace it immediately, and then take up the matter with your contract manufacturer to prevent future problems.

Listen. Stay connected with your retailers and listen to what they have to say. Ask questions: "How are things going? What are your problems? How can we better serve you? What's missing? What's new?" Check in regularly by phone and e-mail. Meet face-to-face with buyers or store owners whenever you can. Visit the stores; see for yourself how your product is being displayed, how customers are responding to it, and how it stacks up against other products. Talk to the store manager and store clerks, and ask for their opinions, observations, and advice. I visited our local retailers that carried Hot Picks and talked to them all the time.

Stay current. Stores change and markets change. To keep retailers and consumers happy and loyal to your brand, you have to stay ahead of the curve and come out with new and improved products. Pay attention to emerging trends in your niche, your industry, and in the world in general, and pay extra-close attention to what's going on with your retailers. Talk to them and to anyone who might help you come up with great products your retailers and consumers will love. When we were designing our Girls Rock line of Hot Picks, I asked my daughter, Elizabeth, to help me because she knew what girls her age liked and what the latest trends were. Hot Picks were the best-selling small musical accessory at Walmart because of her input! So listen to whomever can help you stay up with the trends.

• • •

If you follow these simple practices, not only will stores and consumers keep coming back, but they'll spread the word . . . and you'll get into other stores and add new customers. It will also be a lot easier and faster to expand your brand and bring new products to market because you'll have an army of retailers and consumers waiting with open arms.

Managing the Monster

W HEN YOU'RE in startup mode and intensely focused on getting your product developed, protected, made, marketed, and sold and keeping those first hard-won customers happy, it is easy to let your business just manage itself. Often, it's all you can do to figure out the cash and product you've got coming in, going out, and on-hand. But at some point, your business gets big, busy, and complicated enough that somebody has to step up and steer the ship, before it starts taking on water or going under. If you're like most inventor-entrepreneurs, the management wheel is in your hands and yours alone. Even if you have a partner or can hire a business manager to share the load, you're still the captain. It's still up to you to run a tight ship and navigate your business through the turbulent growth years.

That means sitting down on a regular basis—weekly, monthly, quarterly, however often is needed—and analyzing all the different aspects of your business:

- How are things going on the financial end?
- Is your bookkeeping up to date?
- How is your cash flow?
- Are you having trouble paying bills?
- Are you getting paid on time?
- Are your insurance premiums, licenses, and taxes up to date?
- How are your day-to-day operations going?

- Do you have any persistent problems or delays with your manufacturing?
- Do you have control of your inventory, or are you overstocked or continually running short?
- Are customer orders being shipped on time?
- Is your website up-to-date?
- Are you stoking the social media fires?
- Are you consistently marketing your product, and is that effort working?
- Are you adding stores or losing accounts?
- Are your manufacturer's reps doing a good job?
- Are your sales revenues going up, going down, or going nowhere?
- Are your retailers and distributors happy?
- Are you keeping tabs on what's going on in the market and in your industry?
- How near or far are you from the vision, mission, objectives, strategies, and action plans you laid out on your one-page business plan?
- Are you heading in the right direction, or do you need to adjust course or change your plan?

You have to set time aside to break it down and deal with each aspect. If you run into a situation that you don't know how to deal with, do some research and ask for help. Figure it out. Let's face it: most of us learn as we go, and we all have times when we're just flying by the seat of our pants. That's okay; it comes with the territory. It's also okay to make mistakes; everyone does. Just learn from them. Find a successful entrepreneur or small business owner and ask how he or she handles issues when they arise. Find someone to mentor you.

When we started Hot Picks, there was a lot about running and managing a business that I didn't know. As the company grew, I was able to learn about all the different parts of the business. I had to break down the work into different compartments and develop a plan of action for each. I'd make a chart of all the tasks I needed to do and how I was going to tackle each. Some of the action items were short-term, some were long-term, and some were immediate.

I suggest you do the same: look at every part of your business, figure out what needs to be done, and develop a plan to tackle all the different tasks and projects in each area of your business. Write it down, whether on a chart, spreadsheet, whiteboard, sheet of paper, or your iPad. Revisit and update your action plan often. Start each day by looking at the plan and deciding what needs to be addressed that day.

Taking Care of Business

You need to manage every area of your business. All areas are important, and they are all integral. If something goes askew in one area, that can affect other areas. It all needs to work well in order for your business to succeed.

First and foremost, effectively managing your business is about ensuring that you consistently provide great product and great customer service. Whatever it takes to do that, do it.

These are the other critical components of managing a product-based small business:

- Leadership
- Business relationships
- Quality management
- Inventory management
- Financial management

If you're doing a good job in these areas and you've got great product and customer service, you should be able to keep your business on track and moving in the right direction.

Where You Lead, They Will Follow

Sooner or later, as your business grows, you will have to hire employees. Managing people is different from managing a process or project. When we started Hot Picks, I had very little experience managing people, and it hurt me. I didn't really understand what the job encompassed; I could barely manage myself. I wasn't a great manager, in part, because I wasn't a very good leader.

I've since realized that being a good leader is the key to being a good manager. A good manager leads by example. A good leader inspires people. What I'm learning today is that inspiring people to follow you is a much greater task than simply guiding and supervising people.

Every employee is an ambassador for your business, representing you and your brand. You want the people answering the phone, shipping orders, and keeping your books to really care about what they are doing and to feel like it's their company, too. That sense of accountability doesn't just happen. You need to inspire it. You have to give employees a reason to feel that way. Show them you care—about your work, your business, your customers, your vendors, your product, and your employees.

First, you have to hire the right person for the job, which means you have to understand what you need and want from that employee. Finding the right employee is more art than science. The most important thing is to find someone who fits with your company and with your personality and management style. When I'm hiring an employee, I always look for someone who has certain qualities that can't be found on a résumé: a good attitude, character attributes that are similar to mine and the company's, an open mind, a good work ethic, honesty, a willingness to learn, the ability to admit to mistakes and move on, and the desire to succeed.

I also prefer to find someone through referrals. In my opinion, that is the best way to find a great employee. Ask friends, colleagues, or someone within your industry (e.g., contractors and vendors). Just because you have a referral does not mean you don't need to check references. *Always* check them!

A lot of people are finding employees through social networking sites, such as LinkedIn. Some use an employment agency or website, or a temp agency. Wherever you find potential employees, check their references, and do more than one interview.

I've noticed that people who are a little older (in their forties, fifties, or sixties) seem to have a better work ethic and are on time more often than the younger generations. Our workforce at Hot Picks was people in their fifties and sixties. They worked hard and long and were very reliable. If you do hire people who are younger, make sure they are fresh out of school so you can train them properly.

Don't hesitate to hire someone with a completely different background than your own. Sometimes, that person looks at things differently, and having a different perspective is beneficial to your business.

If you hire the wrong person, it's in your best interest to sever the relationship as soon as possible. I'm not talking about firing someone because he or she makes a mistake; there's always a learning curve and transition period, and you should always give people the chance to fix their screw-ups. But sometimes a person just doesn't work out, and no one benefits from prolonging the problem. Sometimes it's best to cut ties early. Letting a problem hire linger on can make it even more difficult to dismiss the employee later.

At Hot Picks, we had regular employees as well as seasonal contract labor, which we used only when we had a spike in orders. We just called those people in when we needed them.

I've found that the best employees are self-starters who don't need you to motivate and micromanage them. Still, as a manager, you need to communicate to the employee what your expectations are, and then give her or him the encouragement, support, and opportunity to excel and to grow. You may also need to groom some people. I had to do that with several employees. So make sure whomever you hire is willing to learn and to work as part of a team. Give everyone, including yourself, time to grow.

Keep the Relationship Fires Burning

Business relationships are somewhat like a marriage: the real work begins and the real love comes after the honeymoon is over. Just because a retailer fell in love with your product and the first few orders went smoothly doesn't mean you can just sit back and watch the checks roll in. Just because your contract manufacturer bent over backward to get your product and packaging right and the first few runs have gone off without a hitch doesn't mean you can ignore them and expect them to never go astray. Absence does not make a business relationship stronger any more than it makes the heart grow fonder. Every important business relationship you have—with customers, vendors, manufacturing reps, partners, investors, bankers, and mentors—needs your attention, and some need tender loving care.

I think it is especially important to meet face-to-face with your manufacturers every once in a while. It's not just about talking to the person in the head office. It's also about communicating with the folks on the production line. You really want to establish relationships with the people making your product day in and day out. Walk the line. Shake hands. Get to know them. If you are meeting with the suits in the head office, wear a suit. If you are meeting with the people on the line, dress like them. The last thing they want to see is another "suit" checking them out.

Reach out to all your business associates as often as you can. Engage them in conversation. Ask what you can do for them. Let them know they're important to you. Thank them. Listen to them. You'll learn things that will help you manage and grow your business. You'll build an army of supporters that will make your job easier and your company more successful.

The ABCs of TQM

In corporate America, *total quality management* (TQM) is a set of fancy policies, practices, and tools used to ensure that every product and service is delivered to customers with no flaws, defects, fumbles, delays, or mistakes. Of course, 100 percent perfection is impossible for any company to achieve. Mistakes happen. Stuff happens. But the nut of TQM—taking deliberate actions to assure, control, and improve quality—is a great concept you can use to better manage your business. Mess-ups cost money. They take time and resources to resolve. They can damage or destroy relationships. If left unchecked, they can really hurt your business.

Fortunately, there are simple ways to manage the quality of your product and customer service.

To assure quality, you can develop a great product, test your product, pick a good contract manufacturer, and set up a reliable supply chain. You can hire good customer service people and train them well, and maintain an ongoing dialogue with your retailers, distributors, consumers, and employees so you can anticipate and prevent quality control problems. It's also really important to have a good product specification that spells out the required quality standards and the return policy if those standards are not met. Both parties must understand, agree to, and sign off on that written agreement.

To control quality, you can work in partnership with your contract manufacturer, freight forwarder, warehouse, and order fulfillment team to set up policies and practices that enable you to catch and correct mistakes before product is shipped to customers. You can have a QC person on the production floor and/or at the port to spot-check inbound shipments from your manufacturer. You can record all instances of late shipments, short shipments, defective products, customer returns, customer complaints, and so on, and then periodically review them to identify repeat offenses and failure patterns that need to be addressed at a higher level.

To improve quality, you can establish customer service policies and procedures that enable you to identify and remedy problems quickly and efficiently. You can establish a good return policy and make it easy for customers to make a complaint or suggestion. You can solicit feedback from your retailers, distributors, and consumers and take it seriously. You can make sure customer calls, e-mails, and social media posts are handled by a real person and any corrective action is taken promptly.

Managing quality will save you money, headache, and heartache.

Product In, Product Out

Managing inventory is a delicate balancing act. You want enough product on hand so you can fill orders immediately, but you don't want to pay to produce, ship, and store any more product than you can sell before your cash starts running out. The more stock-keeping units, or SKUs, you have, the more retailers and distributors you have, and the

THE HIGH COST OF LOW QUALITY

Annette Giacomazzi/CastCoverZ

Getting the right people on board is so important, even if you have to pay a premium, because then you don't have as many problems. And problems can cost a lot more than a higher wage. It can cost you lost sales and lost customers in addition to the cost of having to correct the mistake.

For example, I had a seamstress who wasn't meeting my standards, and I was getting a tremendous amount of returned product from customers. I did a two-month history of the products she had sewn that had been returned, and it was outrageously unacceptable! The money I was spitting out replacing the defective products and doing damage control to make the customers happy exceeded the expense of hiring someone new who I knew would provide the quality of product I needed. Nowadays, the day-to-day operations are getting easier and easier because I'm hiring the right people and vigilantly controlling quality.

bigger your customers are, the harder it becomes to keep that balance. Hot Picks had so many different picks at one point that it became difficult to manage. In hindsight, I would have reduced our SKUs a bit so that we didn't have so many different designs to inventory and keep track of.

To ensure you have enough inventory on hand when you need it, you have to anticipate and monitor new customer orders, constantly monitor the flow of product moving in and out of your warehouse, and schedule and adjust your production runs accordingly and carefully.

We started out at Hot Picks doing everything visually. You could walk into our stockrooms and actually see what we had. We eventually moved to a computerized inventory control system, which ran on our personal computers and cost about $3,000. Whatever method you use to record and monitor the products moving in and out of your warehouse (or basement or garage or spare bedroom, as the case may be), just realize that it is important to have an accurate inventory management system that enables you to see what you have coming in, going out, and on hand at any given time. As your business grows, make sure the inventory management system you have in place is still doing a good job. When the time comes, don't wait too long to step up to a more sophisticated system that allows you to maintain the visibility and control you need to make sure your inventory, production schedules, and customer order shipments are all in sync.

You'll need to know your contract manufacturer's lead time so you'll know when to reorder. In a perfect world, by the time your

CHECKING IT TWICE

When Hot Picks started taking off, we had orders coming in over the phone, through our online store, through mailed and faxed purchase orders, through our distributors, even in person. We were shipping all over the world using freight forwarders and all over the country using FedEx, UPS, DHL, and other carriers. We filled all the orders ourselves for a while. Everyone in the company was doing it at one point!

It seems like it would be so easy: an order comes in; you look at it, grab a box, go get the picks off the shelf, pack up the box, and ship it to the customer. It wasn't easy. I was surprised at how hard it was. It seemed like every box we shipped out had something missing or wrong with it. We had retailers calling all the time about it, and that was the last thing we wanted!

At first we had a system where whoever was filling an order would pull the inventory, check off what he or she had pulled, pack the picks in the box, and ship it out. We learned the hard way that we needed to check every order *twice* to make sure it was complete. So we put in a system where one person would pull the inventory and check it, and then a different person would pack it and check it off. The packing slip had check-offs and signatures. Double-checking orders and hiring a young person to fill orders full time solved the problem.

It's very important to your reputation that customers get exactly what they order. So if that means checking each order two or three times, it's worth it. Do whatever it takes to get it right.

production order arrives, your inventory will be down to the minimal amount needed in reserve. But that is very hard to do.

Another way to effectively deal with inventory is to use a fulfillment house to ship your orders. A fulfillment company will store your product, receive orders, package, and ship your product to your consumers for you. You will be charged a storage fee that is typically based on the requirements necessary to store your product (e.g., temperature-sensitive items will cost more to warehouse than items where temperature doesn't matter). Fulfillment companies specialize in this type of service and are a great asset when inventory issues may be a concern.

Another major advantage to using a fulfillment house is it will have storage facilities readily available for your product. There are numerous costs involved in renting your own storage facility. A fulfillment house services several businesses at the same time, which means the expenses are distributed to all companies utilizing the service. Other advantages are reduced shipping costs as well as reduced costs for shipping materials. Fulfillment houses do business in bulk and receive bulk discounts.

If you decide to explore this option for your inventory and shipping needs, keep in mind the fulfillment house becomes your shipping center. You won't have control over the shipping process and handling procedures, and the customer will ultimately look to you to fix any errors. As with anything in your business, be sure you have done some research to find a reputable fulfillment company. A reference from someone you know and trust is always best.

Cash Flow: Staying Alive

Ideally, you'll always have enough cash in your coffers to pay your bills and employees, to handle unexpected costs and losses, to fund innovation and expansion, and to keep you going for a while if revenues take a nose dive. That's not always the case, though. In fact, many inventor-entrepreneurs put so much money into bringing a product to market that they are left with limited funds to run and grow the business. Being cash-strapped is the most common nemesis of startups and early-stage businesses. No matter how well funded your company may be, you'll need to be careful about how and when you spend whatever money you have in reserve. To stay alive, you'll also need to carefully manage your cash flow.

Cash flow is simply the movement of money into and out of your business. Cash flow management is ensuring that you always have enough money coming in (receivables) to cover the money going out (payables). Managing cash flow can be tough. But there are simple strategies you can use to make it easier.

The main goal of cash flow management is to speed up the time it takes you to turn:

1. Materials and supplies into products
2. Inventory into receivables
3. Receivables into cash

One of the, if not the, most important objectives of cash flow management is to reduce or eliminate the lag time between when you have to pay suppliers and when you receive payments from customers. The main strategies for achieving that objective are to delay the outlay of cash as long as possible and to encourage anyone who owes you money to pay as rapidly as possible.

To do any of that, you need to have a handle on how much money you've got coming in and going out, where it's coming from and going to, and when you can expect to receive it or dole it out. That's why it is critical to prepare monthly or even weekly cash flow projections and analyze them carefully to identify potential problems.

A cash flow projection is an accounting of the amounts and dates of:

- Scheduled cash receipts—money you *know* you're going to receive at a specific time, such as interest
- Customer payments—an educated guess based on invoices that are coming due and the customers' payment history
- Bad-debt collections, reimbursements, and other sources of incoming cash—an educated guess based on historical data and recent/current collection efforts and internal business activities

- Payments due to vendors—contract manufacturers, materials suppliers (production, packaging, shipping), freight carriers and forwarders, graphic designer, web designer, industrial designer, PR agency, and so on
- Cash expenditures—an educated guess on cash outlays for office supplies, travel, equipment (when not purchased on terms), inventory (when not purchased on terms), and so on
- Operating expenses—rent, utilities, salaries and wages, taxes (sales, income, employees), advertising, marketing, membership dues, insurance, licenses, professional fees, and so on
- Debt payments

Keeping close tabs on your cash flow will help you manage your inventory by enabling you to better coordinate your production runs with your customer orders. It will also help you to avoid, identify, and resolve a potentially crippling cash crunch. How? Let me show you the ways.

Improving Receivables

Here are some commonly used strategies to facilitate the flow of cash into your business:

- Require credit checks on all new customers. Extend credit terms only to customers with a good credit rating. For customers with a poor credit rating, require cash on delivery (COD) or advance payment (at time of order) via credit card or cashier's check.
- Offer discounts for early payments. The most common is 2 percent less if paid within 10 days. Make sure to cite the standard "net" terms as well—for example, "2/10, n 30."
- Require a down payment at the time an order is placed—typically, 20 to 50 percent of the balance due.
- Issue customer invoices promptly—ideally, the same day an order is shipped; always within two to three days.
- Track accounts receivables weekly to identify and address any delinquent payments. If a payment is more than a week late, follow up immediately. Continue to follow up regularly (no more

than once a week) until payment is received, up to 90 days. After 90 days, it's time to take more serious collection actions.

- Generate quarterly and annual accounts receivables reports, and review each customer's payment history. Identify any chronically slow-paying customers and decide whether the delinquencies are serious enough and negatively impacting your cash flow to take some kind of preventive action, such as requiring COD on all future orders.
- Liquidate all outdated inventory. Do this periodically, running a special promotion for a short period of time (say, 30 days), offering big discounts on product that's been sitting in your warehouse or storeroom for too long.

Sometimes, for the sake of your long-term relationship with a good customer who normally pays on time, you need to be flexible and give that customer a little more time. These days, 45 or 60 days is not uncommon, and you may even allow really good customers to go 90 days in a pinch, provided you have the cash reserves to do it.

Managing Payables
Here are some strategies that will help you to better control expenditures:

- Track your accounts payable activity regularly (monthly, if not weekly). If you see expenses growing faster than sales (receivables), monitor your spending closely, examine your costs carefully, and reduce spending and cut costs wherever possible.
- Order product only when you really need it to fill customer orders and to maintain the minimal amount of product in inventory to handle returns and special small orders.
- Take advantage of creditor payment terms. If one offers you a discount to pay early and you can afford to do so, then take advantage of the discount. If a creditor gives you 30, 60, or 90 days to pay, then take full advantage of the time to generate enough income to pay on time.
- Use electronic funds transfer to have the payment transferred from your bank account to your creditor's bank account on the

last day the payment is due (e.g., exactly 30 days from the date of invoice).

- Pay on time all the time. Then, if you do run into a cash crunch and can't pay on time, contact your creditor immediately—before you're in arrears. Offer to pay some of the balance now, even if it's a small amount, and ask for a little more time to pay the balance. Doing so builds trust and understanding. Never avoid your creditors; always take the initiative to work with them to pay your bills.

- Ask for flexible payment terms. If you have a large order that you cannot pay all at one time, ask to make reasonable payments.

When You Are Running Low or Out of Cash

In the beginning, until you have enough sales to have a steady flow of cash coming in and to build up your cash reserves, you may run into a cash crunch now and then . . . or for a while. That's when you need to cut or defer any noncritical expenditures. But often that's not enough to give you the cash you need to buy necessities that you can't buy on credit and to pay your bills on time. You also don't want to get in arrears—and in bad graces—with your vendors, suppliers, and other creditors. You certainly don't want to get a big order from a plum customer and not be able to fill it because you don't have enough inventory and don't have enough cash to order product from your manufacturer.

So if you're running low on cash or fear you might run out, you need to get the money you need to stay alive *before* you run out of cash. Here are some ways to help you do that:

- Ask your suppliers for extended terms—for example, 45 or 60 days, rather than 30 days. Some vendors may even agree to 90 days on a one-time basis. This is like getting a short-term, no-interest loan.

- Ask your best customer(s) to accelerate payments, and offer a discount for early payment.

- Ask late customers to pay on accounts that are 90 days or more past due. Give a discount if they pay now.

- Arrange for a line of credit from your bank.
- If you have a loan or line of credit, ask your lender if you can make a partial payment or even skip a payment.
- Use a factoring company (a financial services company that floats you the money on your receivables). A factorer will pay you 80 to 85 percent of your receivables immediately and collect the money from your customers for you, keeping 15 to 20 percent of your receivables as its commission.

Asking vendors for extensions once in a while is fine—as long as you contact them before your account goes into arrears and they agree to it. But habitually paying late and not bothering to communicate with them when you know you're going to be late puts you in bad graces with your vendors and makes it more difficult to manage your cash flow.

Most big retailers won't agree to any payment terms other than their own. The best candidates for cash-only and COD sales are small retailers.

DOING WHAT COMES NATURALLY
Linda Jangula/Wiki Wags

I've been in the pet business all my life and showing beagles competitively since I was five years old. My passion is making dogs and their owners happy. My business is an extension of that, not the other way around. So I've structured my business to enable me to focus on the things I enjoy most.

A factoring company handles our credit checks, billing, receivables, and payments now, so we don't have to worry about that anymore and it frees up a lot of time for us. It can really be a life saver, too, if our receivables aren't in but we need to pay our manufacturer.

We have a fulfillment center that does our bulk shipping. They could take care of our smaller orders, too, but we prefer to handle those because it gives us an opportunity to connect with pet owners and small pet stores. We hear such wonderful stories from them!

The Bottom Line

At the end of the day, it's all about the bottom line: Are you able to pay your bills? Do you have the funds to build and grow your business? Are you earning more than you're spending? Are you putting any money in your pocket? Yes, passion is an incredible driving force. It feels great to create a product people actually want, buy, and enjoy. Starting a business from scratch is an accomplishment to be proud of.

It usually takes time to create a successful, profitable business. But you have to at least know whether you're on the verge of collapse and whether all your blood, sweat, and tears are moving you in the right direction, toward not only emotional but also financial reward.

The simple fact is, you cannot effectively manage a business if you're not managing your finances. To do that, you need to know:

- How much money are you spending, and what are you spending it on?
- How much money are you earning daily, weekly, monthly, and annually?
- Are revenues fluctuating, decreasing, increasing, or holding steady?
- How much money are you carrying in receivables?
- How much cash do you have in reserves?
- Are your bills being paid on time?
- Are customers paying you on time?
- What is your gross profit margin?
- What is your net worth?

Managing your finances begins with keeping up-to-date financial records and generating financial documents that provide the information you need to gauge the financial health of your business. That means you'll probably need to hire a bookkeeper and/or accountant at some point, whether on a full-time, part-time, or contractual basis. You'll certainly need to generate and review monthly financial reports, such as a balance sheet, cash flow statement, and profit and loss (income) statement.

To Forecast or Not to Forecast
Is Not in Question
Craig Wolfe/CelebriDucks

I don't do forecasting in the way of business flowcharts. . . . I can't even read those kinds of documents. How could I set them up? I don't even think about it. But I can tell you how much money is in the bank, to the penny, without even looking at my account. I don't look at it. I just have this sense of how much money I can spend and how much not to spend.

I don't worry about net 30 or net 60, either. I pay vendors immediately. I treat people the way I want to be treated.

Paying and Getting Paid on Time

You'll also need to make sure you're paying your vendors on time and your customers are paying you on time. Asking vendors for longer payment terms, say 60 days instead of 30 days, or for extensions once in a while is fine—as long as you contact them before your account goes into arrears and they agree to it. But habitually paying late and not bothering to communicate with them when you know you're going to be late puts you in bad graces with your vendors and makes it more difficult to manage your finances.

As for delinquent receivables, it's a reality all businesses have to deal with. You can reduce the risk of delinquent accounts by having all new customers fill out a credit application and then doing a credit check and background check to make sure they pay their bills on time. Even with that, you're still going to have customers who occasionally or routinely do not pay on time.

Remember that sometimes maintaining good relationships with customers who normally pay on time can require being flexible with your payment terms on an occasional basis. I don't recommend making this a normal practice, but to keep a good customer, it may be necessary from time to time.

For chronic late payers, you have two choices: (1) start a serious collection process and stop taking orders from them; or (2) take only cash on delivery (COD), requiring them to pay in advance by credit card, PayPal, or a cashier's check from a bank.

Some small businesses are selling product only on a cash basis, which is something to consider for smaller retailers. Most big retailers won't agree to any payment terms but their own; it's basically *their way or the highway* when it comes to payment terms. If you do offer or require cash-only payment terms, make it easy for them to pay, for example, online with PayPal or over the phone with a credit card. Be aware that you'll pay a small fee for that.

To give retailers and distributors an incentive to pay on time and/or in advance with cash, consider offering a small discount (2 percent net 10 days).

Gross Profit Margin

People often ask me what their gross profit margin should be. That depends on the age and size of your business and on the type of product and its price point. For the first couple of years, a small business may have a small gross profit margin or even run at a small loss and still turn out to be a successful, profitable business. If your business isn't at least breaking even after two years, you should really evaluate what you're doing and maybe talk with a consultant or your mentor to figure out what you might do to increase profits.

Once you're past startup mode, a gross profit margin of 20 to 25 percent is reasonable for very large, expensive products. For the kind of smaller consumer goods that comprise most of the products brought to market by inventor-entrepreneurs like you and me, a 40 to 50 percent gross profit margin is desirable.

Be Careful What You Wish For

Hot Picks had a booth at the largest North American music industry tradeshow, NAMM, and we were working it, giving away thousands of picks all day long. Our booth was so small and so mobbed with people that we had to push our tables into the aisles to conduct meetings. A lot of buyers came through, most in the morning, when it was quieter and less crowded. Early the second morning, a guy came into the booth and was looking around. I could tell he was interested but he wasn't saying much. I treated him with respect and got to know him a bit during the show. It turned out he was a manufacturing rep looking for five or six products he could bundle together and present to Walmart. Hot Picks was one of them.

The rep got us into Walmart, and sure enough, Walmart was interested. We were blown away. At the time, we were in thousands of stores across the United States and the world, so we weren't new at this. We were in some large chains, too—but not Walmart. This was the big time. This was the game changer. How much so we could never have imagined.

We had a wide range of picks. The Walmart buyer selected which designs the company wanted to carry and was very smart about it. She chose a good variety: our Girls Rock line, some Disney designs, and some skulls. Our first shipment sold so well that Walmart started buying directly from us. Even though we were shipping directly to Walmart, we were still using the manufacturing rep, so we continued to pay him his 10 percent commission.

Becoming a Walmart vendor took a long time and a lot of paperwork. The company wanted to know everything about us and our business and how we could fit into its very specific system—everything from packing our stuff in the right-sized boxes to shipping codes. If an order wasn't done exactly to Walmart's specification, the company would ship it back for us to fix and resend, which meant the product was not delivered on time, which was a major problem. We had to be very careful. Each of the chains and big-box retailers Hot Picks was dealing with did things a little differently, and at times it was challenging to keep up with all the different specs.

Finally, we were approved as a Walmart vendor, and we waited to get our first order, unsure of what to expect. We weren't asked for a full national order at first. The plan was to test 200 or 300 stores at a time. For us, that would be a really big order. How do you prepare for that? We weren't ready. I don't think most people are. We were shipping out of a very small location and had only a few employees. We were shipping to individual stores, so the orders were never too large. We had worked out our shipping kinks and had a system in place that worked well for our other accounts. But a Walmart order was completely different.

I tried to prepare by talking to other businesses about how they handled big orders. I did some math and tried to estimate potential volume. We at Hot Picks had an idea, but Walmart didn't tell us explicitly what was coming, nor were we told when. All we knew was that we had two weeks to ship the order once it came in. Fortunately, our manufacturer was in the United States, so I knew we could have product in two weeks. But still, how would we ship it? I started breaking down what a $200,000 or $300,000 order would mean. How many picks? How many clamshells? How many boxes? What did we need to fill an order like that? The list I put together shocked me. I knew it would change our company dramatically.

I looked at the timeline and determined how long it would take us to get each component we needed, such as labels, boxes, clamshells, shipping material, and how much output one worker could do. That wasn't difficult to estimate. I did underestimate a little, of course. It wasn't a problem to get the picks on time, but we needed a larger space than we had to house them. Our office was too small, but we weren't ready to move yet because we didn't know what to expect. That's when I should have asked someone who was a Walmart vendor what it was like. I didn't do that.

I estimated how many picks a pallet could hold, how many pallets we'd need, and how many trucks it was going to take. We were going to need 20 pallets of raw materials! I decided to rent a big storage unit, put the pallets in there and pull from them when we needed to send orders. For some reason, I didn't get the spatial dimensions right at all. You have to be able to walk around pallets, and I had assumed we would just stuff them in there. The space was way too small. We had to have a couple of rental units to store the material. It was mind-boggling to see.

Then we realized we would need an army of people to put all those guitar picks into clamshell packages. I looked at the math again and started to panic. We did not have the requisite workers to put this together fast enough. How could we get this order out? We also had to start planning for the second and third orders! We had to be really creative. We did not want to lose this account.

I realized it was going to take 100 people, working three or four days, to get the order out in two weeks. We had a network of people whom we would give product to and they would come back with the work done. It went well for large orders. We even had pick parties sometimes. People would come over and build inventory. But 100 people? This was too big for that arrangement. That's when my wife came up with the brilliant idea that her school could do it; we would donate money to special causes at the school. Teachers, parents, and kids could get into it over the weekend. So I rented a truck—I can barely drive a sports utility vehicle—and loaded it with product. We assembled everyone, easily more than 100 people, to pack the picks. Two days later, we had a lot of product. I lost a lot of weight those two weeks. The parents of my assistant, James, also had a lot of friends work in their garage over that same weekend. It took a massive effort, but we got it done.

It took a lot of planning, which hadn't worked, but we learned from our mistakes. We learned we needed a warehouse and labor force. We had to start planning for the second order. Once this machine starts up, it's not going to stop; hopefully, it doesn't stop! I rented a warehouse in town, and we started to hire contract labor to build inventory. We brought in 20 people, day in and day out, building product for the next order.

When the first semi pulled up to our office park, the truck got in okay and we loaded it up, but at 53 feet, it didn't go out very easily. I think he damaged the bushes a bit, but he did get out. That's when we knew we had to find a new way to ship product. All of this was just to supply Walmart.

Walmart has a tracking system for its vendors, where you can track your sales daily. Our product was selling, and it was exciting to watch. It was also very helpful. When Walmart places an order for your product, you need to be ready to ship it—or you won't be its vendor for long. You have to constantly track how much of your product Walmart has in stock and how much you have in stock. This information is important to know so you can place a production order, if need be, to make sure you have the inventory to fill the Walmart order when it comes in. That's the scary part, because you have to build inventory ahead, and Walmart takes 60 to 90 days to pay. If you have to pay your manufacturer before then and you don't have enough cash in reserves, what do you do?

This is when you may need to play the money-float game, by using a factoring company, getting a bank loan or line of credit, or floating your own money. We had to pay our manufacturer in 30 to 45 days. We considered using a factoring agent because we knew the big production order could put us in a cash flow crunch very quickly. I also went to Bank of America with the Walmart purchase order and asked the bank to loan us the money, which it wasn't wild about. Luckily, we were able to float our own money. We managed, and Walmart always paid.

It was an exciting time, and seeing our product on the giant's shelves was awesome. We did extremely well and were the best-selling product in the small music accessory category with Girls Rock. But being a Walmart vendor took a herculean effort and caused a lot of stress because we had to greatly scale up our business. It changed the business for me. I was no longer being creative or working on advertising and marketing. I was managing a business with employees. I had to sit at a desk all day every day, managing the company—making sure we could supply product, making sure everyone was doing his or her job, making sure everyone got paid, and making sure we got paid.

Another downside to being a vendor for a giant retailer such as Walmart is that if it suddenly stops selling your product, you can be left with a lot of excess inventory. The key is to not put all your eggs in the giant's basket and to have other channels of distribution to sell the product if that were to happen.

As challenging and scary as being a Walmart vendor can be, it can also be very rewarding. To deal with the challenges, I read a lot and asked people for help to transition from a guy who created products and sold them to small music stores to an entrepreneur running a full-on company and selling to Walmart. It felt great to think about how I'd gone from packing picks into boxes with my wife and kids at our kitchen table to having 30 workers packing picks in a warehouse and Walmart trucks pulling up. I learned. I grew. I enjoyed it. But it's not what I'd set out to do. It was an amazing experience that I'm grateful for. But it's not what I wanted to do.

That's what you need to be careful of.

I think most inventor-entrepreneurs want to be a Walmart vendor, but you have to be aware that it's going to greatly affect your business—and you. It takes you to a completely different level, and you're going to be doing things you never had to consider at the beginning of the business. You have to manage a full-scale business. You have to be comfortable with all that that entails. Is that what you want? The size of your company is going to determine how you spend your time and what you do. Maybe you'll find someone to manage it for you, but if it's your company, you're going to have to take on that responsibility, at least at first.

You can grow into something you really don't want to be. You can create a monster. So be aware, take one step at a time, and learn as much as you can throughout the experience.

MAXIMUM VALUE BRAND EXPANSION
David Mayer/Clean Bottle

I've built up a distribution channel for an eco-friendly plastic water bottle with lids on both ends that screw off for easy cleaning. That distribution channel is an asset that is as valuable as the product. Our new water bottle holder, The Runner, and stainless steel water bottle, The Square, opened up the market even more. But I don't do products just for the sake of doing products. I think a lot of companies come out with new low-quality products just because they can. Then, all of a sudden, they have an inferior brand, and someone else comes along with something better. At the end of the day, you've got to look at where you start to get diminishing returns. You need to add value, not just new product, to your brand.

When the Going Gets Tough

For most inventor-entrepreneurs, managing and growing a business is like going to the School of Hard Knocks, day after day, for the first few years. You're going to make mistakes, things aren't always going to go the way you've planned, and your business is going to be affected by things over which you have no control, such as the economy. Stress can come at you from every direction, and it can be overwhelming. That's why it's so important to really believe in your product and enjoy what you're doing. That makes it a lot easier to come back every day and resume the battle.

This journey is not for the weak of heart, that's for sure. You come out of the gate really passionate and excited only to get knocked down again and again. It's tough to wake up in the morning and pump your fist in the air if, for the last six months, you haven't been able to get any real sales, your money is whittling away, you're losing confidence in your product, and you're wondering what you're doing here. When that happens, you need to be able to dig deep and recharge yourself. Creating a successful business takes more than managing your business. It also takes passion, drive, and guts.

Remember, too, that no bad day or single blunder is going to bring down your company, so focus on the long term. Accept that you're going to have ups and downs, and so is your business. Learn from reading and from other people who are running small businesses. Get involved in the community of entrepreneurship. Never stop learning, and plan out as far as you can. Start with a day, and then a week, and then months out! Keep on revisiting and editing your business plan, but have the future in mind.

Cruise, Expand, or Sell

Some people start a business with the intention of getting it launched and profitable, and then kicking back and letting it run on autopilot. That's a fast track to nowhere. When you cruise, you snooze and you lose. But if it's more downtime you're after, that might be possible . . .

GROWING TO SELL
Amy Baxter/Buzzy
I think that, ultimately, we will be acquired by someone. Because of that, I'm much more focused on increasing our sales than on increasing our profit margin. Right now, the demand for our product is fairly inelastic; to the people who need it and the places that want to sell it, it is very reasonably priced. So now the goal is to get wide enough distribution that we can get a real sense for what the market saturation is.

eventually. If your business is doing well, and you continue to innovate for the market, and you've put the right people and practices in place, you can kick back a little (or a lot) and let them wear some of the hats you'd rather not wear anymore. But I don't think that's cruising.

A lot of entrepreneurs are itching to expand their brand. I think you have to be careful about expanding your business into new areas. We tried to expand into areas other than picks, such as straps and guitars. We also expanded by taking on new licenses, such as our Disney license. Some of it worked and some of it didn't. We even considered adding drumsticks to our brand. Even though drumsticks are in the small music accessories category, they don't appeal to the same market as guitar picks. It didn't cross over. It would have been like starting a completely new business, because the customer was different.

So be careful how you expand. Make sure you're not getting into the wrong area. Licensing other characters and celebrities, like Disney and Taylor Swift, worked because it was still about our core business. We appealed to a different lifestyle, which worked. We increased our audience. I sold the company right when we started selling guitars; but it was the same. We weren't in the business, and there were some huge players. We were going to have to spend a lot of energy and time to be successful.

Analyze how much work an expansion might require, including an entirely new and different strategy. Make sure it's really the right fit.

You're going to dilute your resources, time, energy, and finances into this new expansion, so make sure it's right. In hindsight, I question our decision to do straps as well as sticks. But at the time, we wanted to increase the orders we got by offering other products. People need only so many picks.

A lot of experts advocate growing your business with the intention to sell it—even if that's not really your intention. This is pretty interesting. If your goal is to sell your company one day, you have to set up your business in such a way that it doesn't require you. Your brand and your business need to be able to exist without you. Should you grow tired of running the day-to-day operations or want to move on or retire, someone else should be able to take over your company and run it successfully. So, regardless of what your plans for the company and for your future are today, as you move forward in the months and years to come, I think it's a good idea to put things in place to make your business capable of operating and succeeding without you. How you set up your business and build your brand is almost like creating a playbook that someone else can follow in your absence. So be mindful of that in everything you do.

I sold Hot Picks. I was never even planning to go into business, so I had never planned to sell it either. I loved every part of it: working with the bands, having a presence and friends on Myspace, the letters we received from fans, working the tradeshows. There was not one part I didn't enjoy, and I think it showed. We always made our business about our customer first. In doing so, we built a loyal brand. Everyone loved us because we loved them. My partner, Rob, saw that one of my other technologies was taking off, and he realized it was time for me to move on. He wanted to take charge of the business, and I was ready to hand over those reins. I was the CEO, and he had let me lead, even though we were partners. Rob bought out my share of the company, and he's done a fantastic job with Hot Picks, which celebrated its tenth anniversary this year.

• • •

Starting your own business can be a very rewarding experience. To have complete control of the whole process—from coming up with a great simple idea and bringing it to market, to marketing your product and building brand loyalty, to building a team and a business, to managing day-to-day operations, to expanding your brand and growing your business, to preparing to hand over the reins to someone else or sell your business—can be the most exhilarating and terrifying journey in your life. It's what being an entrepreneur is all about, and you never know where it may lead you.

I am currently on my third adventure as an entrepreneur with Accu-Dial. It's a startup, and I sold my Spinformation label patent portfolio to the company. I now serve as CEO of Stephen Key Design, an affiliate of AccuDial, and report to the board of directors of AccuDial, on which I also sit. I would not have been able to embark on this journey had I not had the experience of starting and running a small business. It all began with a simple idea that I sold at street fairs and in my own retail store, which led to launching a business to bring another simple idea—changing the shape of a guitar pick—to market, where it was sold by retailers all over the world, including a giant, Walmart. I loved every part and every minute of it. And everything I learned then I am using today.

So here's my advice: start small, keep it simple, grow slowly, and structure your company in such a way that you can hand it off to someone else, if and when you're ready. Regardless of where you end up, you, your brand, and your business will be the better for it. Meanwhile, enjoy the journey!

Appendix

Valuable Resources

For web links, addresses, phone numbers, and additional resources, visit the Resources page on the Stephen Key website (http://www .StephenKey.com/resources). Among the many resources available on the page are the following.

Books on Patents

On the Resources page on my website, you will find the patent books I highly recommend you have on your bookshelf, including those written by David Pressman, a patent attorney. There are many other great books on patents that you can read to learn more about patents and other intellectual property protection tools and issues.

Business and Motivational Books

Over the years, I've read many good books that might help you out. For a list of business and motivational books I recommend, including my all-time favorite, *The Magic of Thinking Big*, visit the Resources page on StephenKey.com.

Business Plan

A business plan is a formal statement of your set of business goals, why you believe those goals are attainable, and your plan for reaching those goals. Refer to the Resources page for a sample business plan and for addresses of websites that can provide additional help.

Company Phone Numbers

I have found WhitePages.com to be the most useful and accurate tool for looking up the phone numbers of companies in the United States. You'll find a link to WhitePages.com and several other websites, as well as search techniques you can use to find company phone numbers, on the Resources page.

Contact Names

Getting your foot in the door or getting advice about something along the way will be much easier if you have the name of someone to contact. LinkedIn.com, LinkedIn.com "groups," and Jigsaw.com are great websites to look up and communicate with specific contacts at companies. You can search these sites by company name and job title.

Crowdfunding

The Jumpstart Our Business Startup (JOBS) Act, which was recently signed into law, legalizes crowd funding for business ventures. Crowdfunding, usually done via the Internet, is a collective of people who network and pool their money and other resources to help fund a project they deem worthwhile. Other names for this kind of funding are crowd financing, equity crowdfunding, or hyper funding. For more information, visit my Resources page.

Engineering Associations

When you're developing your idea and need expert advice on a certain aspect of its design, trade associations are a great place to find creative people with technical expertise. Several engineering associations are listed on the Resources page on StephenKey.com.

Entrepreneur Websites

There are many websites that are useful to product developers and entrepreneurs. StephenKey.com continually maintains a list of these sites on its Resources page, as they are always changing and growing.

Foreign Patent Offices

Most industrialized countries have a patent office. For a complete list of patent offices around the world, visit the Resources page.

Freight Forwarders

A freight forwarder is a person or company that organizes shipments from the manufacturer location to the destination point. Businesses use freight forwarders for shipments within the United States and internationally. Visit the Resources page to see a list of freight forwarders.

Free Business Counseling

The Small Business Administration (SBA) is a great place to get free general business advice. Visit the Resources page to get the latest link to the SBA's small business planner website as well as the phone number to the organization's answer desk.

SCORE (Society Core of Retired Executives) is another organization that offers free business counseling. Former retired executives volunteer their time to offer business advice.

If you know what kind of help you are looking for, both the SBA and SCORE can help; however, if you don't, you probably won't get much out of these organizations. Some SBA and SCORE counselors can be very helpful, but you will need to ask for the specific type of help you are seeking in order to get to the right person. Otherwise, you'll just get a brochure and the standard advice everyone else gets.

Fulfillment Houses

A fulfillment house is a company that specializes in inventory control and order fulfillment. Fulfillment companies offer to store your product, receive your orders, package your product, and ship the item(s) to your consumers. For a listing of companies who offer these services, please visit my Resources page.

Government Programs for Inventors

The National Technology Transfer Center (NTTC) links U.S. businesses with federal labs and universities that have the technologies, facilities, and researchers they need to maximize product development opportunities.

The U.S. Department of Energy Efficiency and Renewable Energy (EERE) invests in clean-energy technologies that strengthen the economy, protect the environment, and reduce dependence on foreign oil. Get the latest links from the Resources page on StephenKey.com.

Grants

Grants are funds disbursed by grant makers to a recipient. In order to receive a grant, some form of written document is required describing the purpose or project for which the funds will be used. This document is often referred to as a proposal. A completed application form is usually required as well. For help in learning how to write a grant proposal, visit the Resources page for links to websites.

Industrial Design Firms

Industrial design firms are available if you need help improving the aesthetics, structure, and usability of your product. They can also be beneficial if you need to improve the marketability of your product. For a list of industrial design firms, visit the Resources page on StephenKey.com.

Intellectual Property

Patents, copyrights, trademarks, and trade secrets are all considered intellectual property. On my Resources page, you will find the critical links you need to learn more about protecting your intellectual property, from the U.S. Patent and Trademark (USPTO) website to the Library of Congress website.

Inventors' Associations

For a comprehensive list of inventors' associations, groups, and clubs around the United States and abroad, visit my website's Resources page. These resources are great for educational purposes, for getting help with your ideas, and for connecting with other independent product developers.

Invoice

An invoice, also commonly known as a bill, is a commercial document issued by a seller to the buyer. It indicates the products, quantities, and agreed prices for products or services the seller has provided to the buyer. The payment terms are also listed on the invoice. Visit my website's Resources page to see a sample invoice.

Mail Order

Mail order, or direct mailing, is when a consumer buys goods or services by mail delivery. The consumer places an order in some remote fashion, typically either via phone or on a company's website, and the business ships the merchandise directly to the address supplied by the buyer.

A mail order catalog is a publication that contains all of the general merchandise offered for sale by a business. There are numerous websites that support mail order catalogs, where you can post your merchandise and reach a wide range of consumers. For links to these sites and more information on mail order, visit the Resources page on StephenKey.com.

Major Retailers

For an up-to-date list of major retailers and how to find them, visit my website's Resources page.

Manufacturing Directories

If you need to research how to manufacture your idea or to get quotes on the cost of manufacturing your idea, StephenKey.com has a list of free manufacturing directories on its Resources page that will help you out tremendously.

Marketing

Marketing refers to the processes of creating, communicating, and delivering a product of value to customers and clients.

Business-to-consumer marketing is the process of establishing strong customer relationships by creating value for customers such that they want to return to purchase your product.

You should devise a marketing plan that identifies your target market and focuses on the needs of that target market. Take a step back and try to be objective in anticipating the wants and needs of consumers from a consumer viewpoint. A marketing strategy should be developed to effectively manage the promotion of your product in the marketplace. There are numerous ways to promote your product. Some things to consider when promoting your product are packaging, branding, creating a website, creating pages on social media websites, and writing press releases for free media advertising. Marketing doesn't have to be an expensive venture, but it is necessary to get your product seen by your target market.

For valuable marketing information and links, please visit my website's Resources page.

Nondisclosure Agreement (NDA)

A nondisclosure agreement (NDA) is a legal contract between at least two parties that creates a confidential relationship between the parties to protect any type of confidential and proprietary information or trade secrets. Other common names used are confidentiality agreement (CA), confidential disclosure agreement (CDA), proprietary information agreement (PIA), or secrecy agreement. To see a sample NDA, visit my website's Resources page.

Package Design Firms

Package design firms are businesses that deal with the science, art, and technology of protecting products for distribution, storage, sale, and use. Professional firms are also capable of dealing with the process of design, evaluation, and production of packages. A comprehensive list of package design firms can be accessed on the Resources page of StephenKey.com.

Patent Attorneys

The USPTO's website lists every patent attorney and agent licensed to practice in the United States. For the current link to this list, visit my website's Resources page.

Patent Research

For most people, downloading individual patents using Google Patents to research "prior art" will be sufficient. The Resources page on StephenKey.com gives you the link to Google Patents, which you can use to download patents completely free.

However, if you are doing some serious patent research and need to download several patents, you might consider using patent downloading software. On the Resources page is a list of both Macintosh and PC software to manage this process for you.

Press Releases

A press release, news release, media release, press statement, or video release is a written or recorded communication directed at members of the news media for the purpose of announcing something newsworthy. Press releases are typically mailed, faxed, or e-mailed to editors at newspapers, magazines, radio stations, television stations, and/or television networks. There is a sample press release on the Resources page on StephenKey.com, along with valuable links to help you learn how to write a press release.

Point-of-Purchase Displays

Point-of-purchase displays can be used in retail environments or at trade shows. These displays are marketing tools that are created to catch buyers' attention and draw them in for a closer look. Sizes of POP displays vary from small to large and are an effective way to advertise your product. The Resources page has a listing of places to purchase a POP display.

Prototypes

People who make prototypes go by different names, including model makers, industrial designers, rapid prototyping specialists, 3D print-makers, CAD designers, machinists, and computer animators ("virtual" prototypes). Which one is right for you depends on the type of prototype you need (if you need one at all). For more information on what each type of prototyping specialist does and on how to find people with these skills, visit my website's Resources page.

Provisional Patent Filing Software

There is actually a computer program that walks you through the process of filing your own provisional patent application (PPA). I use such software and have found that it really helps speed up the process of filing a PPA. Visit my website's Resources page to learn more about your options for filing your own PPA using software.

Purchase Order

A purchase order (PO) is a commercial document issued by a buyer to a seller. It indicates types, quantities, and agreed prices for products or services the seller will provide to the buyer. To see a sample purchase order, visit my website's Resources page.

Raising Capital

Loans, crowdfunding, and grant writing are definitely ways to raise capital for your business, but there are several alternative avenues you can use. Angel investors and venture capitalists are part of what is known as equity financing. These types of investors will want part ownership of your business, but you don't have to pay them back immediately. This arrangement allows you to focus on your product rather than on paying back a loan immediately. You can also consider bootstrapping, royalty financing, business incubators, reverse merger, private placements, asset sales, or ask friends and family to help fund your venture. Refer to the Resources page on StephenKey.com for links that discuss all of the ways to raise capital.

Retail Buyers

Finding a retail buyer can be difficult because major chains seldom share buyer's contact information. You can pay for the names and phone numbers of buyers through companies such as The Chain Store Guide or The Salesman Guide. The lists vary in price, but usually start around $200. If you live in a larger city, you can probably find these guides on the shelves; however, you won't be able to check the materials out, so plan on spending a little time researching while you are there. For more information, visit the Resources page.

Retail Packaging

Retail packaging can include anything used to surround the product being sold. Whether you choose a box, clamshell, or bag, your packaging should protect your product against physical damage, and also should be visually appealing to consumers. The Resources page has an extensive list of packaging companies for you to review.

Sell Sheet, or Cut Sheet

Many times, you don't need to make a prototype. A sell sheet, or cut sheet, provides a virtual tour of your product. Sometimes, if you can illustrate the benefits of your product in a sell sheet, you can make the prototype later, after you get some interest. Visit my website's Resources page to see a sample sell sheet.

Setting Up Your Business

A company name, business structure, dedicated phone number, and e-mail are all important things to think about and set up. Before choosing a company name, you should understand trademarks, service marks, corporate names, and the importance of not choosing a name already in use. You will also need to decide what legal form your business will take: sole proprietorship, partnership, limited liability company (LLC), C-corporation, or S-corporation. The things to keep in mind when choosing a legal structure are liability, double taxation, and ownership. Each state has different requirements, so it is best to consult with your attorney before making your final decision. Doing some homework and understanding the differences between these legal forms will give you a better idea which form your business should take. Visit the Resources page for more information.

Shipping Order

A shipping order is an inventory control document that is used to identify what should be shipped from the warehouse and to whom and where the product should be delivered. A sample shipping order is available on my website's Resources page.

Shopping Search Engines

Shopping search engines are a great way to do research. They are a little different than regular search engines in that the search results are based on products available for sale on the Internet. You should use a shopping search engine every time you come up with a new idea. It is easy and will likely provide some valuable information. Google Product Search is one of our favorites; get the link by visiting the Resources page on StephenKey.com.

Trade Show Directories

You'll find links to several tradeshow directories on my website's Resources page. These directories are certain to include at least one trade show for a product, product category, or industry that fits with your idea.

United States Patent and Trademark Office

The United States Patent and Trademark Office (USPTO) is the governing agency responsible for establishing patent law in the United States; it issues all patents in this country. The agency has many people ready to assist you. It even has an Inventors Helpline to answer your questions. On the Resources page on StephenKey.com you'll find all the direct links and phone numbers to the most important resources the USPTO has to offer, from fee schedules to patent searching and beyond.

Work-for-Hire Agreement

A work-for-hire (WFH) agreement is a written contract that outlines the work to be created by an employee as part of the job or as a contractor on behalf of a client. A WFH specifies all terms and conditions of the agreement, including project specifications, deadlines, and payment. All parties agree in writing to the WFH agreement. According to copyright law in the United States and certain other copyright jurisdictions, if a work is "made for hire," the employer, not the employee, is considered the legal author. A sample WFH agreement can be found on my website's Resources page.

Index

About the Author

STEPHEN KEY has been a successful entrepreneur and award-winning product developer for more than 30 years. He has licensed more than 20 of his ideas and holds 13 U.S. patents. His products have been sold in major retailers throughout the world and have been endorsed by basketball great Michael Jordan and *Jeopardy!* host Alex Trebek. Together with his partner, Andrew Krauss (president of Inventors' Alliance), he formed inventRight, LLC, which mentors and teaches entrepreneurs and inventors.

Stephen's first book, *One Simple Idea: Turn Your Dreams into a Licensing Goldmine While Letting Others Do the Work* (McGraw-Hill), was released in February 2011. It was number one on Amazon Small Business Marketing at the time it was released, and over a year later it still held that number one position and had more than 150 five-star ratings. The book is being translated into six different languages.

In October 2011, Stephen Key Design, LLC and the rights to use Stephen's patent portfolio were acquired by AccuDial Pharmaceutical, Inc. Stephen now sits on the board of directors of AccuDial, is the chairman of the IP Committee, and is chief executive officer of the division that sells his patent portfolio of Spinformation Rotating Labels (http://www.spinlabels.com). Products utilizing Stephen's patented technology won Product of the Year Award in Canada and also Gold and Bronze at the 2011 Edison Awards. AccuDial products that utilize Stephen's technology have also won the 2011 New Product Innovation Award from Frost & Sullivan, as well as the PTPA Seal of Approval.

Recognized as an outstanding leader in the field of innovation, Stephen has appeared on national television numerous times, including an appearance on the CNBC show *The Big Idea with Donny Deutsch* and as an expert guest on *Dr. Phil*. He was also a consultant on the first season of the hit ABC reality TV show *American Inventor*, created by Simon Cowell. Stephen has been interviewed by national magazines, newspapers, and authors such as Tim Ferriss (*The 4-Hour Workweek*) and Donny Deutsch (*The Big Idea*).

Stephen has been happily married to his beautiful wife, Janice, for 23 years. They share their home in the creative capitol of the world (Modesto, California). The Keys have three children. Their oldest daughter, Madeleine, graduated from the University of California, Berkeley, in May 2011, where she earned her bachelor's degree in peace studies and conflict resolution. Their son, Jonathan, is currently attending U.C. Berkeley, where he is pursuing a degree in history. Their youngest daughter, Elizabeth, attends the University of Oregon, and is studying to earn her degree in psychology.